Quick to Knit ™

Great Gifts

PURSES, PILLOWS, MITTENS & MORE

S0-BYW-967

Publications International, Ltd.

DESIGNERS: Ann Berez (page 50); Chrissy Gardiner (pages 36, 56, 74);
Laurie Gonyea (page 40); Judith Horwitz (page 53); Megan Lacey (page 83);
Shirley MacNulty (page 80); Vanessa Montileone (page 92); Amy Polcyn (page 78);
Lucie Sinkler (page 88); and Beth Walker-O'Brien (pages 44, 47, 60, 62, 66, 71)

TECHNICAL EDITOR: Jean Lampe
ILLUSTRATOR: Joni Coniglio
PHOTOGRAPHY: Ron Hines/Silver Lining Digital, Inc.
PHOTO STYLING: Sheila Scatchell/Sheila Styling
ADDITIONAL PHOTOGRAPHY: © Deborah Van Kirk (page 4)

Copyright © 2006 Publications International, Ltd. All rights reserved.
This book may not be reproduced or quoted in whole or in part by any means whatsoever
without written permission from:

Louis Weber, CEO
Publications International, Ltd.
7373 North Cicero Avenue
Lincolnwood, Illinois 60712

Permission is never granted for commercial purposes.

ISBN-13: 978-1-4127-1340-5
ISBN-10: 1-4127-1340-4

Manufactured in China.

8 7 6 5 4 3 2 1

Contents

36

Knit Wise! 4

Simple Stripes Felted Bag 36

Mittens and Headband 40

Herringbone Belt 44

Curlicue Scarf 47

Chevron Pillow 50

Striped Wine Sack 53

Ribby Socks 56

Ripple Scarf 60

Gull Stitch Toque 62

78

Himalayan Silk Purse 66

Zigzag Throw 71

Checkered Pot Holders 74

Mermaid Scarf 78

Mohair-look Hat 80

Bulky Boot Socks 83

92

Bias Bag 88

Fluffy Fun Pillows 92

Designer Directory 96

Knit Wise!

So you've been wanting to learn to knit? Look no further than these simple step-by-step instructions with clear, easy-to-follow illustrations. *Quick to Knit™: Great Gifts* is the perfect tool for any first project, and it gives you tons of fabulous options. Your only dilemma will be choosing which to make first! Read on—you'll be hooked in no time.

Casting On

The cast-on row is the foundation row of knitting. There are many ways to cast on stitches. One method may be easier for you to do, or it may work better for certain techniques, such as buttonholes. Try each of the following cast-on methods, and start with the one that most appeals to you. *Note:* The cast-on should be as elastic as the body of your knitting. If needed, the cast-on may be worked using a needle two or three sizes larger than your gauge needle. Knit the stitches onto the smaller needle as you knit the first row.

Making a Slipknot The first stitch on your needle for most cast-on methods is a **slipknot**.

Step 1: Hold the yarn in your left hand about 8" (20cm) from the end. With your right hand, make a circle with the yarn *(fig. 1a)*. If it's helpful, hold the circle between your index finger and thumb to prevent it from slipping.

Making a Slipknot

Fig. 1a

Fig. 1b

Fig. 1c

Step 2: With the working yarn behind the circle, insert the knitting needle through the circle from front to back and catch the working yarn, pulling it through the circle to form a loop *(fig. 1b)*.

Step 3: With the new loop on the needle in your right hand, gently pull both ends of the yarn (the tail and the working yarn attached to the ball) beneath the needle, then pull on the working yarn to tighten the new loop so that it fits snugly around the needle *(fig. 1c)*.

Cable Cast-on This cast-on is especially good when you need a firm edge. Work loosely, without pulling the stitches too tight.

Step 1: In your left hand, hold the needle with the slipknot. Hold the working yarn in your right hand. Insert the right needle through the slipknot from front to back and wrap the yarn around the right needle from back to front *(fig. 2a)*.

Step 2: Pull up a loop with the working yarn, creating a new stitch on the right needle. Insert the left needle tip into the new stitch *(fig. 2b)* and slip it onto the left needle. There are now 2 stitches on the left needle. *Note:* To prevent the

Cable Cast-on

Fig. 2a

Fig. 2b

Fig. 2c

Fig. 2d

cast-on edge from becoming too tight, insert the right needle from front to back between the 2 stitches on the left needle before tightening the yarn. Gently pull the working yarn to tighten the stitch.

Step 3: With the right needle in position between the 2 stitches on the left needle, wrap the yarn around the right needle as shown *(fig. 2c)*, and pull through a new loop.

Step 4: Using the tip of the left needle, slip the new stitch from the right needle as before *(fig. 2d)*, and slip the right needle out of the stitch.

Repeat steps 3 and 4 to cast on additional stitches. End with step 4 to complete the last cast-on stitch.

Long-tail (or Slingshot) Cast-on The benefits of this cast-on method are that it's quick to do and makes an elastic edge. Both working yarn and tail are used. The tail length should be roughly three times the width of your desired cast-on, or about 1" (2.5cm) per stitch for worsted weight yarn, plus several inches extra for the yarn tail allowance to weave in later. If you underestimate the length of yarn tail needed, pull out the work, add more yarn to the length, and begin again. Or, begin the cast-on using two balls of the same yarn: One serves as the tail, and the other is the working yarn. Tie the ends together in an overhand knot, leaving about a 6" (15cm) tail, make the slipknot as usual, and then begin the cast-on. When the cast-on is completed, cut one of the yarns, leaving about 6" (15cm), and begin to work with the other. When the garment is finished, untie the overhand knot and weave in the loose ends.

Step 1: Place the slipknot onto the needle in your right hand, with the yarn tail in front (closest to you) and the working yarn (attached to the ball) behind the needle. Pull the working

LONG-TAIL (OR SLINGSHOT) CAST-ON

Fig. 3a

Fig. 3b

Fig. 3c

SIMPLE CAST-ON (BACKWARD LOOP CAST-ON)

Fig. 4a

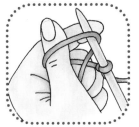

Fig. 4b

Fig. 4c

yarn taut over the left forefinger, and wrap the yarn tail around your thumb from front to back. Secure both the working yarn and the tail between the remaining three fingers of your left hand and palm. Place the forefinger of your right hand on top of the slipknot to hold it in place *(fig. 3a)*.

Step 2: Insert the needle under the yarn in front of your thumb, working from front to back and pulling the yarn slightly upward *(fig. 3b)*. Insert the needle over the yarn on your forefinger, moving from top to bottom so the working yarn lies on top of the needle to form the new stitch.

Step 3: Pull the needle toward you through the loop on your thumb as you remove your thumb from the loop *(fig. 3c)*. At the same time, pull down on both pieces of yarn, tightening the stitch by pulling on the tail, keeping the stitch firm and even but loose enough to slide easily.

Simple Cast-on (Backward Loop Cast-on) This cast-on is probably the easiest to learn, but it doesn't have a neat edge like other cast-ons. Use it when working a few cast-on stitches or on button-holes. This cast-on tends to grow longer and become less manageable as you work the first row of knitting because the cast-on stitches tighten, making it difficult to insert the needle.

Step 1: Place the slipknot on a needle with the yarn tail in back and the working yarn in front. Hold this needle in your right hand.

Step 2: Wrap the working yarn over your left thumb from back to front. Secure the working yarn between the third finger of your left hand and palm to add tension and hold it in place *(fig. 4a)*.

Step 3: Insert the needle under the yarn looped around your thumb, working from bottom to top *(fig. 4b)*. Pull up on the needle a little as you slide the yarn off your thumb and onto the needle.

Knit Loops and Purl Loops

Before you venture any further, look at these six illustrations. They will help you understand many things about knitting, so study them well and plan to return to this page often. When a cast-on or stitch pattern specifies working into the front loop or back loop, simply match the instruction to the illustration to see exactly which part of the stitch is being described.

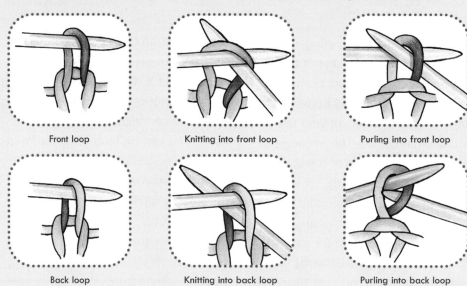

Front loop	Knitting into front loop	Purling into front loop
Back loop	Knitting into back loop	Purling into back loop

Step 4: Gently pull on the working yarn to tighten the new stitch on the needle *(fig. 4c)*. Repeat steps 2–4 to cast on as many stitches as desired. End with step 4.

Knitted Cast-on This cast-on is easy to work and is very similar to the cable cast-on *(see page 5).* The difference between the cable cast-on and the knitted cast-on occurs after the first stitch is made.

Step 1: Place the slipknot on a needle and hold the needle in your left hand, with the working yarn in your right hand. Insert the right needle through the slipknot from front to back.

Step 2: Wrap the yarn around the right needle from back to front and pull up a loop, creating a new stitch on the right needle *(see fig. 2b, page 5).* Insert the left needle tip into the

CROCHET CHAIN CAST-ON

Fig. 5a

Fig. 5b

new stitch. Both needles remain in the new stitch.

Repeat step 2 for each new stitch until all cast-on stitches are made. Withdraw the right needle after the last stitch is made. Although both needles remain in the new loop at all times, the stitches collect on the left needle only.

Crochet Chain Cast-on The crochet chain cast-on and a standard bind-off look the same: a horizontal chain of stitches. Therefore, it's a good idea to consider this method when making scarves, afghans, baby blankets, and anything else where the cast-on and bind-off edges are visible in the finished item.

Step 1: Place the slipknot on a crochet hook and hold it in your right hand.

Step 2: Take the working yarn in your left hand, placing the knitting needle over the working yarn and under the crochet hook.

Step 3: Yarn over the crochet hook (*see page 18 for yarn over instructions*), draw a loop over the knitting needle and through the slipknot (*fig. 5a*), and take the working yarn under the needle (1 stitch on knitting needle, 1 loop on crochet hook).

Step 4: *With the working yarn under the knitting needle and the crochet hook over the needle, yarn over the crochet hook and draw the yarn through the loop on the crochet hook (*fig. 5b*), and take the working yarn under the needle (1 new stitch on needle, 1 loop on crochet hook).

Repeat from * until the required number of cast-on stitches are on the needle, slipping the last stitch from the crochet hook onto the needle.

The Basic Stitches

Knitting has two basic stitches: the knit stitch and the purl stitch. After you master these stitches, you'll find that you'll be able to create many stitch patterns.

Knitting is enjoyed all over the world, but not everyone likes to knit in the same style. There is no right or wrong style of knitting. This book presents one of the more common knitting methods used in the United States: the American-English method, in which the working yarn is held in the knitter's right hand.

Holding the Yarn Experiment with the way you hold the yarn. Weave the yarn through your fingers as shown, or try other ways until you find a method that works for you. The ability to tension the yarn as it flows through your fingers while knitting will allow you to maintain your gauge and work neat, even stitches. As you become comfortable with it, you'll also see that it's less tiring on the hands.

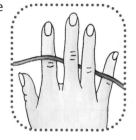

Holding the Yarn

Knit Stitch The knit stitch is the most common and versatile stitch of all. It is smooth on one side and bumpy on the other. The smooth side of the knit stitch is generally used as the right side of the work—the side that faces out. The working yarn is always held behind the needle when making the knit stitch. In other words, the knit fabric and the needle will always be between you and the working yarn.

Knitting every row creates garter stitch *(see page 13)* in flat, back-and-forth knitting.

Step 1: Hold the needle with the cast-on stitches in your left hand. The working yarn is already attached to the stitch closest to the needle tip. Holding the empty needle in your right hand, take hold of the working yarn with your right hand, and hold it behind the right needle. Insert the empty needle from front to back through the first stitch on the left needle *(fig. 6a)*. The right needle is behind the left needle.

Step 2: Bring your right hand and forefinger toward the tip of the right

KNIT STITCH, AMERICAN-ENGLISH METHOD

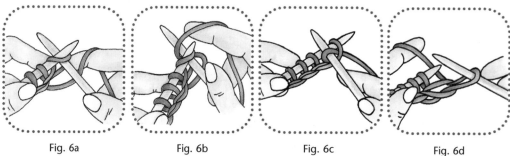

| Fig. 6a | Fig. 6b | Fig. 6c | Fig. 6d |

needle (the yarn is underneath the right needle). Wrap the yarn around the right needle from back to front *(fig. 6b)*. Be careful not to wrap it around the left needle, too.

Step 3: Keeping the yarn firmly tensioned in your right hand, bring the right needle toward you, pulling a new loop through the old stitch *(fig. 6c)*.

Step 4: With the new stitch on the right needle, slip the old stitch off the left needle *(fig. 6d)*. Unlike the cast-on, the new knit stitches are held on the right needle.

You have just knit your first stitch! Repeat until all the cast-on stitches have been knit and are on the needle held in the right hand.

Knitting the Next Row The second and all subsequent knit rows are worked the same as the first: Knit each stitch on the needle in the left hand.

Step 1: When you have knit all the stitches from the left needle, turn the work, switching the needle with all the stitches on it from your right hand to your left hand.

Step 2: The working yarn is attached to the stitch closest to the needle tip. Insert the right needle into the first stitch and repeat the knitting steps across the first row, working into each of the stitches of the previous row instead of into the cast-on stitches.

Note: When beginning each new row, be sure the working yarn is beneath the needle holding the stitches and is not wrapped over the needle. If the working yarn is pulled upward, the first stitch will appear as two stitches, with both stitch loops appearing in front of the needle. If you knit both loops as single stitches, you'll increase the number of stitches on your needle. Remember, the front loop of each stitch should be in front of the needle and the back loop behind the needle.

Purl Stitch The purl stitch is the reverse of the knit stitch. The yarn is always held in front of the work when making the purl stitch. As you work this stitch, the bumpy side faces you and the side behind the needle is now the smooth side. When working flat, back-and-forth knitting, purling every row creates garter stitch, just the same as knitting every row. Alternating rows of knit and purl makes stockinette stitch, in which the knit side is the right side and the purl side is the wrong side *(see page 14)*. The purl side of stockinette stitch is called reverse stockinette stitch, which uses the purl side as the right side and the knit side as the wrong side.

PURL STITCH, AMERICAN-ENGLISH METHOD

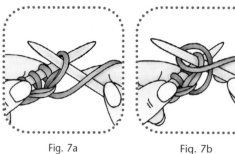

Fig. 7a   Fig. 7b

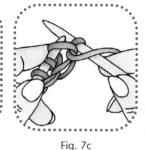

Fig. 7c

Repeat for each new purl stitch.

Purling the Next Row The second and subsequent purl rows are worked the same as the first. Purl each stitch on the needle in the left hand.

Step 1: Hold the working yarn and the empty needle in your right hand and the needle with the cast-on stitches in your left hand. With the working yarn held in front of your work, insert the empty needle from right to left through the front loop of the first cast-on stitch *(fig. 7a)*. The right needle is in front of the left needle.

Step 2: Bring the yarn in your right hand toward the tip of the right needle. Carry the yarn between the needles, wrapping it around the right needle from top to bottom, ending in front *(fig. 7b)*. Be careful not to wrap it around the left needle.

Step 3: Keeping the working yarn in your right hand, use the right needle to pull up a loop, moving backward and away from you through the stitch on the left needle *(fig. 7c)*. With the new stitch on the right needle, slip the old stitch off the left needle.

Step 1: When you have purled all the stitches from the left needle, turn the work, switching the needle with all the stitches from the right hand to the left.

Step 2: The working yarn is attached to the stitch closest to the needle tip and held in front of the work. Insert the right needle into the first stitch with the yarn held in front of the stitches, and repeat the steps of the first row, working into each of the stitches in the previous row instead of the cast-on stitches.

Binding Off This technique finishes the last row and secures the stitches so the needles can be removed. You will often see the phrase "bind off in pattern." This means work the last row of stitches as instructed, and bind off as you work. It sounds tricky, but it's not. The illustrations that follow show a knit row for the bind-off, but it's a good idea

BINDING OFF

Fig. 8a

Fig. 8b

Fig. 8c

to practice the technique on both knit and purl rows.

Step 1: Hold the needle with stitches in your left hand and the empty needle in your right hand. Hold the yarn in position for the knit stitch, behind your work.

Step 2: Knit the first 2 stitches.

Step 3: Insert the left needle from left to right into the front loop of the first stitch on the right needle *(fig. 8a)*. *Note:* This is the stitch farther from the right needle tip.

Step 4: Use the left needle to pull this stitch over the second stitch and drop it off the right needle. One stitch is bound off; the second stitch remains on the right needle *(fig. 8b)*.

Step 5: Knit the next stitch.

Step 6: Repeat steps 3–5 until you have bound off all stitches from the left needle and 1 stitch remains on the right needle. Cut the yarn about 4" (10cm) from the stitch, and pull the yarn tail through the last stitch *(fig. 8c)*. Remove the needle

and pull the yarn tail to tighten.

Many new knitters have a tendency to bind off too tightly. The bound-off edge should be as elastic as the rest of the knitting. If necessary, use a larger needle size to work the stitches in your bind-off row.

Basic Stitch Patterns

Garter Stitch Knit every row or purl every row in flat knitting, and you have garter stitch *(fig. 9)*. It's a great stitch pattern for new knitters because it uses only one simple stitch. Because garter stitch lays flat

GARTER STITCH

Fig. 9

and doesn't curl at the edges, it's often used at the beginning and end of rows to create flat a piece. *Note:* If you knit in the round, either with circular or double-point needles, you'll create stockinette stitch instead of garter stitch.

STOCKINETTE STITCH (KNIT SIDE)   REVERSE STOCKINETTE STITCH (PURL SIDE)

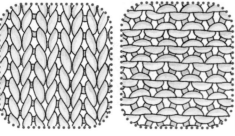

Fig. 10a   Fig. 10b

Stockinette Stitch This is the most commonly used stitch pattern. Simply knit one row, purl the next, and repeat. Stockinette stitch has a tendency to curl at the edges when not stabilized with other, noncurling, stitch patterns, such as garter stitch. Because of that, border stitch patterns are usually added to the lower and upper edges, and the side edges are sewn into the seam.

The knit side of the piece (the smooth side) is called stockinette stitch (fig. 10a), and the purl side (the bumpy side) is called reverse stockinette stitch (fig. 10b). Reverse stockinette stitch is often used as a background for cable patterns because it shows the pattern well.

Ribbing You'll recognize ribbing as the stitch often found at the cuffs and hems of sweaters. It is a very elastic pattern and knits up narrower than stockinette stitch on the same size needles. There are many ways of making ribbing, but the most common are the single rib (fig. 11a) and the double rib (fig. 11b). The single rib is made by alternating one knit stitch with one purl stitch. Double rib is more elastic than single rib and is made by alternating two knit stitches with two purl stitches.

The most important thing to remember when making ribbing is that the yarn must be brought between the needles to the back of the work for the knit stitches and between the needles to the front of the work for the purl stitches. If you finish a row and discover extra stitches, or find a hole in the ribbing several rows later, it's probably because you inadvertently knit with the yarn in front or purled with the yarn in back. This can be easily corrected (see Correcting Mistakes, page 21).

SINGLE RIB   DOUBLE RIB

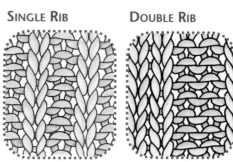

Fig. 11a   Fig. 11b

Ribbing is easy once you learn to recognize knit and purl stitches. Instead of counting stitches, you'll simply knit the knits and purl the purls.

Is That All There Is to It?

You are now a knitter! Practice these basic stitches until you feel comfortable with them, and refer back to the instructions if you get confused.

Use the simple knit and purl stitches to make many wonderful things. But don't stop there! If you keep challenging yourself to try new patterns and learn new techniques, knitting will continue to be an exciting undertaking.

Gauge

The word gauge (or tension) refers to how many stitches (or rows) there are in an inch of knitting using a specific yarn and needle size. The resulting numbers are used to determine how many stitches and rows it will take to achieve a desired size. Remember, the needle size listed in the pattern is the size the designer used to obtain the listed gauge. Two knitters using the same materials may end up with different gauges. A difference of only half a stitch per inch could make a discrepancy of several inches in the size of the finished project. Take time to make a gauge swatch before starting your project—you'll be glad you did. It may be necessary to make several attempts before you achieve the correct gauge.

How to Knit a Gauge Swatch Use the main needle size listed in the pattern. Cast on about 6" (15cm) of stitches, using the stitch gauge given in the pattern to determine the number to cast on. Work the main pattern until the swatch measures 4" (10cm) in length; bind off all stitches. Lay the swatch on a flat, hard surface. Measure, then count

GAUGE SWATCH

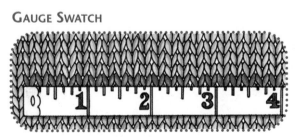

Fig. 12a (20 stitches=4" [10cm])

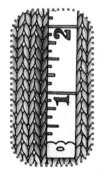

Fig. 12b (12 rows=2" [5cm])

4" (10cm) of stitches across the swatch *(fig. 12a)*. Divide this number by 4 to get the number of stitches per inch. Repeat the process a few times in different areas to confirm the count. To measure the rows, center the measuring tape or ruler lengthwise on the swatch, and count the number of rows over 2" (5cm) *(fig. 12b)* or 4" (10cm) if the pattern is very large vertically. Divide the total by 2 (or 4, if using that number) to determine the number of rows per inch. *Note:* Knit stitches are wider than they are tall; however, in stitch patterns such as stockinette stitch, you'll normally have more rows per inch than stitches per inch. Compare your gauge with the pattern gauge. If your gauge swatch has more stitches per inch than the pattern gauge, this means your stitches are smaller than the pattern gauge, and you'll need to try larger needles until your swatch stitches are the same size

as the required gauge. If your swatch has fewer stitches per inch than the pattern gauge, your stitches are larger than the pattern gauge, and you'll need to try smaller needles to obtain the pattern gauge. Be exact in your measurements, and knit as many swatches as you need, changing needle sizes until you find the size that allows you to obtain the correct gauge.

Knitting in the Round

To avoid sewing seams, you can work in rounds using circular needles or double-point needles.

Circular Needles To work in rounds, cast your stitches on one end of the needle the same as you would on a straight needle. Check to be sure that the cast-on lays flat and smooth and is not twisted. Add an open-ring stitch marker to the end of the needle to mark the beginning of the round *(fig. 13a)*, and work the first round according to your pattern instructions.

Double-point Needles Evenly distribute your cast-on among three or four needles, keeping one needle out to knit with. Be sure the cast-on lies flat and smooth and no stitches are twisted. If you'd like, add

CIRCULAR NEEDLES

Fig. 13a

DOUBLE-POINT NEEDLES

Fig. 13b

a stitch marker to the first needle to mark the beginning of the round. (It's easy for a stitch marker to fall off the double-point needle, so keep an eye on it.) The needles either form a triangle (if you cast on to three needles) *(fig. 13b)* or a square (if you cast on to four needles). With the empty needle, knit all stitches on the first needle. When that needle is empty, use it to knit the stitches on the next needle. Continue to knit the stitches from each double-point onto an empty needle, working the stitches as instructed in the pattern.

Slipping a Stitch

Sometimes instructions tell you to slip a stitch. This means you'll move a stitch to the right needle without knitting or purling. The instructions may indicate whether to slip it as if to knit or purl. **To slip as if to knit** *(fig. 14a),* keep the yarn behind your work and insert the right needle into the next stitch on the left needle as if to knit it. Simply slide the stitch off the left needle and onto the right. **To slip as if to purl with yarn in back** *(fig. 14b),* with the knit side facing you, insert the right needle tip into the next stitch on the left needle as if to purl, and slide the stitch onto the right needle. **To slip as if to purl with yarn in front** *(fig. 14c),* with purl side facing you, slip the stitch as if to purl. When a stitch is slipped using either of these methods, the strand will not show on the knit side of the work. However, some stitch patterns reverse the normal process, so always follow the instructions carefully.

Why does it make a difference how stitches are slipped? When stitches are slipped as if to purl, they are transferred onto the right needle untwisted, which means the front stitch loop remains in front of the needle. When slipped as if

SLIP STITCH

Fig. 14a

Fig. 14b

Fig. 14c

to knit, stitches are transferred in a twisted position so the back loop of the stitch is now in front. Some pattern stitches require this.

A rule of thumb about slipping stitches: Always slip as if to purl unless the pattern instructions specify otherwise. An exception to this rule is that you'll always slip as if to knit when the stitch is part of a decrease method. A stitch that's part of a decrease is transferred to the right needle as if to knit, in the twisted position, because it will later become untwisted when the decrease is complete.

Increases

Increases are used to shape your knitting and to create lace patterns. There are many ways to make an increase; we've listed a few standard methods. Many pattern instructions specify which type of increase to use; others do not. It's important to learn how each increase affects the appearance of your work so you can use the appropriate method. Make small knit swatches and practice each increase method listed here. Label them, and keep them for future reference. Avoid making increases and decreases in the edge stitches, because they affect the

ability to make a smooth seam when finishing. Make increases or decreases at least one stitch in from the edge stitches.

Yarn Over A yarn over is the basis for most lace patterns and is very simple to make. In fact, many new knitters make yarn overs by

YARN OVER

Fig. 15

accident (but in those cases it's called a hole, not lace). When moving the yarn from the front or the back of your work, you would normally be very careful to put the yarn between the needles and not over one (which would create an extra loop on the needle). To make a yarn over when knitting, bring the yarn to the front of the work and then knit the next stitches as instructed (fig. 15). On the next row, work into the front loop of this strand (yarn over) as you would any other stitch, transferring it from the left needle after it is knitted.

Knit 1 in the Front and Back Loops/ Bar Increase This is one of the most visible increases in stockinette stitch: It leaves a little bump that looks like a purl stitch. Use it decoratively or when the

KNIT 1 IN THE FRONT AND BACK LOOPS

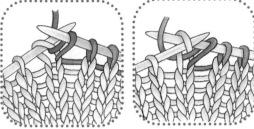

Fig. 16a   Fig. 16b

purl bump is part of a stitch pattern. The bar increase is one of the easiest to make. To make it, knit the front loop, but don't remove the stitch from the left needle (fig. 16a). Knit into the back loop of the same stitch (fig.16b).

Make One These increases are made simply by knitting into the horizontal strand between stitches on the right and left needles. One method creates a left-leaning increase, meaning that the front strand of the increase slants to the left. The other method leans to the right. These are called paired increases.

To make a left-leaning increase:
Step 1: Insert the left needle from front to back under the strand (fig. 17a).
Step 2: With the right needle, knit into the back of the strand (fig. 17b).
Step 3: Slip the strand off the left needle. You now have one new stitch (an increase) on the right needle. Note how the front strand of this new stitch leans toward the left (fig. 17c).

To make a right-leaning increase (see illustrations, next page):
Step 1: Insert the left needle from back to front under the strand (fig. 18a).
Step 2: Knit into the front of the strand (fig. 18b).
Step 3: Slip the strand off the left needle. You now have one new stitch (an increase) on the right needle. The front strand leans toward the right (fig. 18c).

MAKE 1 (LEFT-LEANING)

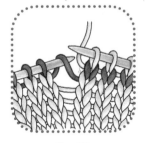

Fig. 17a   Fig. 17b   Fig. 17c

Make 1 (Right-leaning)

Fig. 18a

Fig. 18b

Fig. 18c

Decreases

Use decreases for shaping necklines, making lace patterns, and more. Some decreases have a definite slant either left or right; pattern instructions may specify which type to use. Left- and right-slant decreases are referred to as paired decreases.

Knit Two Together The knit-two-together decrease is made by working into two stitches at the same time. With the yarn behind your work, skip the first stitch on the left needle and insert

Knit Two Together

Fig. 19

the right needle knitwise into the second stitch and the first stitch at the same time, knit the two stitches as if they were one stitch *(fig. 19)*, and remove the stitches from the left needle. This decrease leans to the right on the knit side of the work.

Purl Two Together As the name suggests, this decrease is the purl-side method of the knit-two-together increase. With the yarn in front of your work, insert the right needle through

Purl Two Together

Fig. 20

the loops of the next two stitches on the left needle as if to purl *(fig. 20)*, purl the two stitches as if they were one stitch, and remove them from the left needle. This decrease leans to the right when it is viewed from the knit side of the work.

Slip Slip Knit The slip-slip-knit method is a one-stitch decrease that leans to the left and is usually paired with knit two together on knit rows.

SLIP SLIP KNIT

Fig. 21

Work this decrease as follows: Slip two stitches knitwise, one at a time, from the left needle onto the right needle; insert the left needle tip from left to right into the front loops of both slipped stitches *(fig. 21)* with the yarn in back, knit both stitches together from this position.

Slip Slip Purl The slip-slip-purl method is a one-stitch decrease made on purl (wrong-side) rows. When viewed from the right side of the work it leans to the left and matches the slip slip knit, which is made on knit (right-side) rows. The slip slip purl is usually paired with purl two together on wrong-side rows.

Work this decrease as follows: Slip two stitches knitwise, one at a time, from the left needle onto the right needle (the base of both stitches will be twisted at this point), and slip both stitches back to the left needle in their twisted position *(fig. 22a)*, insert the right needle tip through the back loops of both stitches, entering the second stitch first and then the first stitch, and purl them together from this position *(fig. 22b)*.

IMPORTANT THINGS TO KNOW

You've learned the basics of knitting—but there's always more to learn. This section helps you polish your skills so that your projects have the look of a professionally knitted piece.

Correcting Mistakes

One thing to know about mistakes in knitting is that we all make them. Fortunately, knitting is easily corrected, and you'll learn from any missteps along the way. Once you learn to correct them, you'll be happily on your way again.

Dropped Stitches It's always a good idea to count your stitches often as you work, especially after casting on and after making increases or decreases. This habit will help you catch many mistakes. If your stitch count is less than it should be, it may be because a stitch has dropped from your needle.

SLIP SLIP PURL

Fig. 22a

Fig. 22b

DROPPED STITCHES

Fig. 23a

Fig. 23b

Use a crochet hook to correct a dropped stitch, whether it has dropped one row or several rows (a running stitch).

Step 1: Hold the knit side of the work toward you. Count the horizontal strands between the two needles to determine how many rows the stitch has slipped. It's important to begin with the very first strand closest to the dropped stitch. With the loose horizontal strands behind the loop of the dropped stitch, insert a crochet hook into the loop from front to back. Catch the first horizontal strand and pull it through the stitch *(fig. 23a)*. Repeat the step with each horizontal strand until the dropped stitch is back at the current row.

Step 2: Place the stitch on the left needle untwisted, with the right loop of the stitch in front of the needle *(fig. 23b)*. Continue in pattern.

Joining New Yarn

When you near the end of a ball of yarn, try to change to the new yarn at the row edge. This will prevent the stitches in the middle of your work from becoming uneven, and it will make weaving in the yarn tails much easier, because you can hide them in the seams.

Step 1: Using an overhand knot (to be removed when finishing the item), tie the old and new yarns together close to the needle, leaving a 4–6" (10–15cm) tail on both yarns.

Step 2: Drop the old yarn, and begin knitting with the new one. Once you are more experienced and feel more comfortable with controlling the yarns, you may choose to omit knotting the yarns together and simply drop the old yarn and start knitting with the new strand, tightening and securing the yarn tails later.

Another option is to hold the old and new yarn together and knit with both for a few stitches. Then drop the old yarn and continue with the new. This method attaches the yarn securely and decreases the number of ends to weave in later, but it can leave a noticeable lump, so don't use it in a prominent place.

CHANGING COLORS

Fig. 24

Changing Colors When changing colors somewhere other than the end of a row, drop the old color on the wrong side, pick up the new color from underneath the old, and continue knitting with the new color (fig. 24). This prevents a hole from appearing between colors.

Intarsia Knitting In intarsia knitting the pattern is worked in large blocks of color at a time, and the stitches in each color area are worked from their own yarn supply. Even though intarsia often uses many different colors, it produces a single-layer fabric. In each row, when each group of stitches in one color is completed, that color is dropped (don't cut the yarn) and the next color group of stitches is worked from its own yarn source, either from small individual balls of color that are joined to the work at specific sections or by winding yarn onto bobbins. Always drop the old color on the wrong side, pick up the new color from underneath the old, and continue knitting with the new color.

Making an I-Cord

You can make an I-cord to use as a drawstring, strap, or tie using double-point needles or a short circular needle.

Step 1: Cast on 3 or 4 stitches to one double-point needle. Slide the stitches to the other end of the needle. The working yarn is at the "wrong" end of the needle (fig. 25a).

Step 2: With the yarn strand across the back of the stitches, pull it up to the front at the needle tip and knit the stitches (fig. 25b).

Step 3: Repeat step 2 until the cord is the desired length. Unless instructed otherwise, finish the last row as slip 1, knit 2 together, pass the slipped stitch over. Cut the yarn, and thread the end through the last stitch.

I-CORD

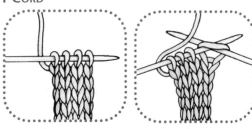

Fig. 25a   Fig. 25b

FINISHING

Most knitters prefer knitting to sewing seams and weaving in ends, but taking care with these final steps ensures that your knitting is shown at its best on both the outside and the inside.

Picking Up Stitches

Pick up stitches using a knitting needle or crochet hook. For a neater edge, use needles or a hook one or two sizes smaller than the working needle. After the pickup is finished, change to the needle size indicated in the instructions. Work with the right side of the piece facing you, unless instructed otherwise. Divide the area of pickup into quarter sections, or smaller spaces if necessary, and mark with pins or thread. This will help you maintain the same number of stitches in each. Example: Pick up and knit 100 stitches. Divide the area into

fourths, and pick up 25 stitches in each quarter section.

If the border uses a different color from the pickup area, pick up the stitches in the main color, then change to the new color on the next row.

Picking Up Stitches Along a Bound-off Edge With the right side of the garment facing you, insert the tip of the right needle into the first full stitch beneath the bind-off row (fig. 26a), wrap the yarn around the needle, and pull it through the stitch, creating a new stitch on the needle. Repeat for each stitch until the required number of stitches are on the needle.

Picking Up Stitches Along a Side Edge With the right side facing you, unless instructed otherwise, join the working yarn at the lower edge if not already attached (see Joining New

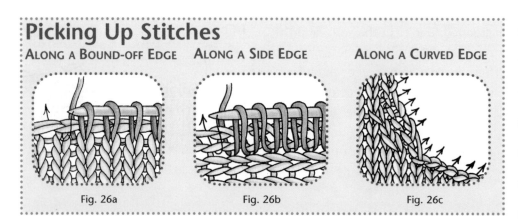

Picking Up Stitches
ALONG A BOUND-OFF EDGE   ALONG A SIDE EDGE

ALONG A CURVED EDGE

Fig. 26a   Fig. 26b   Fig. 26c

Yarn, page 22). Insert the right needle into the fabric through the first full stitch of the first row, and wrap the yarn around the needle knitwise. Pull through a loop, creating a new stitch on the right needle *(fig. 26b)*. Repeat the process, spacing the pickup stitches along the side edge as necessary, but always working into a full stitch. It's important not to leave any holes or uneven spaces in the work.

Picking Up Stitches Along a Curved Edge Curved edges are usually a combination of edges—horizontal, diagonal, and vertical. To pick up stitches along an edge that was formed by making decreases, such as along the neck shaping of a sweater, insert the needle into the stitch below the edge stitch *(fig. 26c)*—not between the stitches—to prevent holes from occurring when the pickup is finished.

Sewing Seams

While it may be tempting to hurry through the finishing so you can finally see the completed project, it's important not to rush through sewing the seams if you want the end result to look polished and professional. Block each piece before assembling *(see Washing and Blocking, page 34)*, and allow the pieces to dry. This helps the edges remain flat as you work.

Shoulder Seams (bound-off edges)

Step 1: Lay both pieces flat, with right sides up. Thread a tapestry needle, and, beginning at the right-side edge of the piece closest to you (the lower piece), insert the needle from back to front through the center of the first stitch. Pull the yarn through, leaving a yarn tail to weave in later.

Step 2: Insert the needle from right to left under the two vertical legs of the first stitch on the piece farther from you *(fig. 27)*, then insert

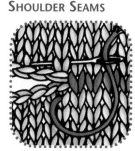

SHOULDER SEAMS

Fig. 27

the needle from right to left under the next two vertical legs on the near piece, beginning in the same hole as the first stitch made. Pull the yarn gently to adjust the stitch and close the stitches.

Step 3: Continue to alternate sides, inserting the needle from right to left under two strands and beginning in the same hole as the last stitch made. Pull the yarn every few stitches to adjust it and close the seam. At the end of the seam, weave in the yarn tail.

Mattress Stitch Mattress stitch is a great stitch to know when it comes to sewing vertical seams, including side and sleeve seams.

Step 1: Thread a tapestry needle with matching yarn, leaving a 4" (10cm) tail to weave in later. With both pieces flat and right sides up, insert the needle under the horizontal strand between the first and second stitches of the first row on one piece and the corresponding strand on the second piece. Gently pull the yarn to tighten.

Step 2: Insert the needle under the horizontal strand on the next row of one piece, and then insert the needle under the strand on the same row of the other piece.

Step 3: Continue to work under the horizontal strands, alternating pieces,

MATTRESS STITCH

Fig. 28

until you have worked six to eight rows (fig. 28), and then pull the yarn gently to close the seam. Continue weaving pieces together to the end of the seam. Weave yarn tails into the seam stitches, and secure.

Whipstitch This illustration shows whipstitch made on flat fabric as a decorative false seam (fig. 29). The same method is also used to actually join two pieces together in a seam, which can be made on the wrong side of the work, or on the right side to create a sporty look.

WHIPSTITCH

Fig. 29

To work flat: With threaded tapestry needle, bring the needle to the front surface (position 1), move the needle upward and to the left of the entry point, insert the needle to the back of the fabric (position 2), exit the fabric to the front (position 3); repeat 2 and 3 until the decoration or seam is finished. Take the yarn to the wrong side of the work and weave it through several stitches to secure.

To seam edge stitches: Align both pieces of fabric with the edges to be seamed next to each other. Insert a threaded tapestry needle from back to front through both edge stitches (position 1), draw yarn through; *move the needle to the left of the first two stitches joined and insert needle from back to front through the next set of edge stitches (positions 2 and 3); repeat from * until all stitches are joined and seam is closed.

Backstitch Backstitch is an easy way to make a firm seam.

Step 1: Thread a tapestry needle with matching yarn. With the right sides together, work along the wrong sides about one stitch in from the edges. Work two running stitches on top of each other to secure the lower edges.

Step 2: With the tapestry needle and yarn behind the work, insert the needle through both layers of fabric about two stitches to the left of the running stitch and pull the yarn to the front of the work.

Step 3: Insert the needle from front to back one stitch back to the right, working through both layers.

Step 4: Moving forward to the left about two stitches, bring the needle to the front of the work, about one stitch ahead of the original stitch (fig. 30). Repeat the process until you reach the end of the seam, working one stitch backward (to the right) on the front side of the work and two stitches forward (to the left) on the back side of the work.

BACKSTITCH

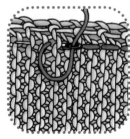

Fig. 30

Step 5: Finish the seam by working two or three running stitches on top of each other, stitching over the bound-off edges. Weave in yarn tails.

Invisible Seam on Garter Stitch As its name suggests, this seam, which also works on seed-stitch fabrics, disappears into the knitting.

Align both pieces of fabric together, matching the top and bottom edges. *Insert the threaded tapestry needle under the top

INVISIBLE SEAM ON GARTER STITCH

Fig. 31

loop of the purl stitch on one edge, pull the yarn through, move the needle across to the adjacent piece of fabric and insert the needle under the bottom loop of the purl stitch on this side, pull yarn through; repeat from * working from side to side to the end of seam. Adjust the yarn tension after seaming several stitches so that each side stitch touches, but doesn't overlap, the other (fig. 31). When the seam is finished, weave in the loose ends to wrong side of work.

THREE-NEEDLE BIND-OFF

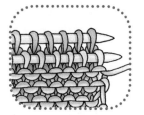

Fig. 32a

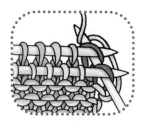

Fig. 32b

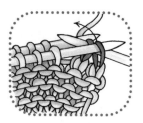

Fig. 32c

Three-needle Bind-off This bind-off finishes off two edges, binding off the stitches and closing the seam at the same time. Normally used to close shoulders, it can also be used to close side seams when working a garment from side to side. You can also pick up stitches along two side edges and then use the three-needle bind-off to close those seams. To make a flat, neat seam on the right side, follow these instructions:

Step 1: With the right sides of the work together, and with the needle tips aligned and facing to the right *(fig. 32a)*, hold both needles in your left hand.

Step 2: Insert the empty right needle into the first stitch on each of the two needles in the left hand, and knit the two stitches together *(fig. 32b)*. Slip them off the needle as you would a knit stitch. You now have one stitch on the right needle.

Step 3: Knit the next pair of stitches the same way. You now have two stitches on the right needle.

Step 4: Pull the first stitch on the right needle over the second stitch (the one closest to the tip), just as you would in a normal bind-off *(fig. 32c)*.

Step 5: Repeat steps 3 and 4 until all stitches have been bound off. Cut the yarn and pull the end through the last loop; weave in the end to secure.

Kitchener Stitch (Grafting) This technique joins live stitches together in an elastic, invisible seam. The method can also be used over bound-off stitches to make a strong, stable seam.

With an equal number of stitches on two needles, and right sides up, hold the needles parallel to each other with points facing right. Thread a blunt tapestry needle with two to three times the length of the area to be joined. For live stitches, work as follows:

KITCHENER STITCH

| Fig. 33a | Fig. 33b | Fig. 33c | Fig. 33d |

Step 1: Insert threaded needle into the first stitch on the front needle purlwise (as if to purl); leave stitch on needle.

Step 2: Insert needle into the first stitch on the back needle knitwise (as if to knit); leave stitch on needle.

Step 3: Insert needle into the same first stitch on the front needle knitwise *(fig. 33a),* slip stitch off needle. Insert needle into the next front stitch purlwise; leave stitch on needle *(fig. 33b).*

Step 4: Insert needle into the same stitch on the back needle purlwise *(fig. 33c);* slip stitch off needle. Insert needle into the next back stitch knitwise; leave stitch on needle *(fig. 33d).*

Repeat steps 3 and 4 until all stitches are worked.

Tip: To make the technique easier as you work, remember this: Front needle—purlwise leave on, knitwise take off; back needle—knitwise leave on, purlwise take off.

Weaving in Yarn Tails

Carefully weaving in the yarn tails makes your knitting look neat and keeps it from pulling loose and unraveling over time.

Thread a tapestry needle with the yarn tail. Working on the wrong side of the knitting, weave the needle in and out of the back of the stitches for a few inches in one direction, and then turn and work in the opposite direction for an inch or two. Pull the yarn gently to tighten, and cut it close to the work. Stretch the knitting slightly so the tail disappears into the last stitch.

Duplicate Stitch

Duplicate stitch is used to create small motifs, make small additions to intarsia, mend socks, and cover knitting errors. It produces a stiff fabric, as stitches are duplicated on top of the knit fabric below. The technique is worked horizontally, vertically, and diagonally.

DUPLICATE STITCH

Fig. 34a

Fig. 34b

For horizontal stitches:

Step 1: Thread a tapestry needle with the same yarn type as the knit fabric beneath. Work with strands about 18" (45.5cm) long to avoid having the yarn plies untwist and fibers shed as the needle is repeatedly drawn through the knit fabric. Rethread the tapestry needle as necessary.

Step 2: Begin the first duplicate stitch in the lower right corner of the motif or pattern. (You'll work from right to left.) Secure the yarn on the wrong side of the fabric, and bring the needle through to the front of the fabric at the base of the first stitch.

Step 3: Insert the needle into the right side of the top of the same stitch, carry the needle and yarn across the back of the work, and bring them to the front on the left side of the same stitch *(fig. 34a)*. Reinsert the needle into the base of the first stitch.

Step 4: Bring the needle up through the base of the stitch to the left of the stitch just duplicated. Repeat step 3.

To work the next row, insert the needle into the base of the last stitch worked, then bring needle and yarn out to the front through the center of that stitch. Turn the work (the motif will be upside down), and work horizontal stitches across the second row of motif stitches, working same as for previous row. Continue working from right to left on each row. Weave yarn tails through the backs of stitches to secure.

For vertical stitches, begin at the lowest point and work upward. Work the same as for horizontal duplicate stitch, but bring the needle out to the front through the center of the stitch above the one just worked rather than the stitch to the left *(fig. 34b)*.

Diagonal stitches are made using a combination of horizontal and vertical methods. Work one stitch horizontally, and instead of finishing by moving to the next stitch on the left in the same row, bring the needle out at the base of the next stitch on the left, one row above.

Chain Stitch Embroidery

Chain stitch is a basic embroidery technique often used to embellish knit

CHAIN STITCH EMBROIDERY

Fig. 35a   Fig. 35b

and crochet projects, as well as fabric. To create flowers, the basic chain stitch is grouped around a center to form petals or attached along a stem to form leaves.

Step 1: Bring threaded needle to the front of the fabric at the first flower petal position. The needle should be at the flower's center, not the outer edges.

Step 2: Move the needle over 1 or 2 threads, insert it to the back of the fabric and back through to the front again at the desired petal length with thread under the needle.

Step 3: Insert needle to back again, catching the flower petal loop as shown *(fig. 35a)*, move the needle upward and to the left, and exit to the front at the position for the next petal.

Repeat steps 2 and 3 for as many petals needed *(fig. 35b)*. After the last petal is finished, take yarn to back and secure the thread by weaving it through several stitches.

Making Pom-poms

Cut 2 circles out of cardboard, each about 1½"(4cm) in diameter. Cut a small hole in the center of each circle; make a slit from outside edge of both circles to the center hole. Hold both circles together with slits aligned. Wind yarn evenly around both circles (going through the slits to the center holes) as tightly as possible. The more times you wrap, the fuller the pom-pom. Cut yarn around outer edges of circles. Cut an 18" (45.5cm) yarn strand, and pulling cardboard circles apart very slightly, wrap strand yarn firmly around pom-pom center a couple of times. Tie strand tightly in a double knot. Remove cardboard circles completely, and fluff out pom-pom. Trim ends to even out if necessary, but do not trim yarn around pom-pom centers. You will use these to attach the pom-pom to your project.

Crochet

Chain stitch and single crochet are frequently used by knitters to create decorative edges, to cast on or bind off, and to make button-holes, buttons, accessory cords, embellishments, and more. Hook sizes are coordinated with knitting needle sizes, but the system for labeling size is different. Crochet hooks

CROCHET CHAIN

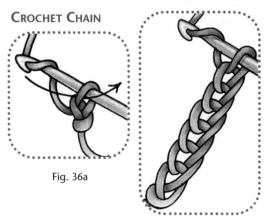

Fig. 36a

Fig. 36b

working yarn *(fig. 36a)*. Pull up a loop, and place it on the crochet hook. Pull both the yarn tail and the working yarn to make the slipknot snug around the shank of the crochet hook.

Step 2: Holding the hook in your right hand and the working yarn in your left, bring the yarn over the hook from back to front, and pull it through the loop on the crochet hook *(fig. 36b)*.

Step 3: Repeat step 2 until the chain is the desired length. When the last chain loop is made, cut the working yarn, leaving a tail to weave in later.

Step 4: Thread the tail through the last chain loop on the hook, and pull to tighten and secure.

Single Crochet Single crochet can be used as a quick and easy finishing edge on your knitted pieces. It is attached either directly to knit stitches, along a bound-off edge, or as a border for other crochet stitches. It makes a firm finish and helps the edges lay flat.

Step 1: Insert the hook under a bound-off stitch (or where directed in the instructions). Bring the working yarn over the hook and pull through a loop, yarn over again, and pull it through the loop on the hook *(fig. 37a)*.

Step 2: Insert the hook under the next bound-off stitch *(fig. 37b)*, yarn over,

are numbered in several different ways. The smallest sizes are steel hooks, which use numbers. The higher the number, the smaller the hook size. Larger hooks are labeled with letters and numbers, A/0 through P/16. Some brands also include metric sizes. Many knitters use a hook one or two sizes smaller than their needle size to prevent the crochet from becoming ruffled or wavy instead of lying flat and smooth against the knit fabric. Practice on your gauge swatch to determine which size hook works best for your project.

Crochet Chain The chain stitch forms the foundation row in crochet. It is quick and easy to make.

Step 1: Begin with a slipknot. Insert the crochet hook into the center of the slipknot from right to left, catching the

SINGLE CROCHET

Fig. 37a

Fig. 37b

Fig. 37c

and pull up a loop (two loops on hook). Yarn over again, and pull the yarn back through both loops on the hook *(fig. 37c)*, leaving one loop on the hook.

Step 3: Repeat step 2 until the required number of stitches is complete. Finish according to pattern instructions.

Double Crochet This stitch is worked into a chain, single crochet, or directly into the knitting, as shown below.

Step 1: Insert the hook into the knitting one stitch in from the edge, yarn over, and pull up a loop. Yarn over again, and pull it through the loop on the hook. Yarn over, insert the hook into the next base stitch *(fig. 38a)*, and pull up a loop (three loops on hook). Yarn over and pull it through the first two loops *(fig. 38b)*, yarn over, and pull it through the last two loops *(fig. 38c)*.

The double crochet is complete; one loop is on the hook *(fig. 38d)*.

Step 2: Yarn over, insert the hook in the next stitch, yarn over, and pull up a loop (three loops on hook). Yarn over and pull it through two loops, yarn over and pull it through the remaining two loops. The second double crochet is complete, with one loop left on the hook.

DOUBLE CROCHET

Fig. 38a

Fig. 38b

Fig. 38c

Fig. 38d

Repeat step 2 for pattern. To end the last stitch, after completing step 2, cut the yarn and pull it through the last loop on the hook.

Washing and Blocking

Always save at least one label from your yarn when you make an item that needs to be washed often. Keep it where you can easily find it. Some yarns can be safely washed in the washing machine and dried in the dryer; others cannot.

If you have any doubt, play it safe—hand wash it.

Fill a sink with lukewarm water (never hot!), and add a small amount of mild soap for delicate knits. Put the garment in the sink, and allow it to soak. Do not agitate or handle roughly. Drain the sink, and gently press down on the garment to squeeze out some of the water. Never wring or twist a wet item; always support the weight so the item doesn't stretch. Fill the sink with cool rinse water; allow the item to soak, drain the water, and again gently press out the excess water. Repeat until the soap is removed.

Spread a layer of thick towels on a flat surface. (Never hang a knitted garment.) Lift the garment from the sink with both hands without stretching it, and spread it out on the prepared surface. Use a tape measure to shape it to the correct measurements. Pin in place using rust-proof T-pins, and let dry.

Some yarns, including wool, can be blocked by using steam, but always check the yarn label first. Lay the garment on a blocking board, and pin it to the correct measurements. Keep the steam spray several inches above the garment—never spray it directly onto the garment.

Felting

Felting is the process of using hot water, agitation, and suds to change (or shrink) a knitted piece into a felted fabric that will not unravel, even when cut. Felting creates a very durable fabric that is practical as well as beautiful.

When making an item to be felted, use extra-large needles and make it several sizes larger than normal. This creates space between the stitches and rows and allows the fibers to shrink while maintaining a smooth fabric surface.

Animal fibers are best for felting. You can use wool, mohair, camel, and alpaca, among others. Superwash wool yarns have been treated to resist shrinking—they will not felt. Synthetic yarns do not felt, either.

To felt, set the washing machine on the hot water cycle and low water level. Add a small amount of dishwashing liquid; too many suds hampers the felting process. Add towels, tennis balls, or washable sneakers to the machine to balance the load and aid the felting process. Allow the machine to agitate for five minutes, then stop it to check the amount of felting. Continue to check every five minutes or so until the stitches completely disappear and the item is the desired size. The amount of felting time varies depending upon the yarn, washing machine, and hardness of water.

Once the desired felting stage is obtained, remove the item from the washing machine, drain the soapy water, and fill the machine with cold rinse water. Soak the item in rinse water for several minutes to remove all soapiness. Set the machine directly on spin cycle to eliminate excess water from the felted item, or wrap it in a large towel and squeeze to take out the rinse water. Remove the felted item from the machine immediately after spinning to avoid wrinkling the fabric. Stretch, pull, and pat it into shape, and allow it to air-dry on a flat surface.

Understanding Knitting Instructions
Like most crafts, knitting has its own language. Knitting patterns use abbreviations, special terms, and punctuation. The language may seem strange at first, but you will quickly master it and be reading patterns like a pro.

Read any special notes or instructions for the pattern you plan to make. When a "finished size" is listed, the numbers given refer to the garment size upon completion (provided you maintain the correct gauge).

Reading through the entire pattern may be confusing at first, so study small sections. Pay attention to punctuation. One sentence usually represents one row; commas and semicolons may mean that something's going to change with the next stitch or row. Instructions inside asterisks, brackets, or parentheses are usually repeated, so look for the directions that explain what to do.

Schematics These are line drawings of the basic garment pieces, to which measurements are added. Usually schematics show the basic measurements before neck ribbing, collars, or other embellishments are added. Check the schematic to determine which size will best fit you in width and length.

Simple Stripes Felted Bag

This generously sized shoulder bag knits up quickly with big needles and a double strand of yarn. Load it up, sling it over your shoulder: This bag looks great wherever you go.

DESIGNER: CHRISSY GARDINER

SIZE

Before felting: about 20×18"
(51×45.5cm)
After felting: about 12×15"
(30.5×38cm)

WHAT YOU'LL NEED

Yarn: 100% wool worsted weight yarn, about 660 yards (604m) main color; 440 yards (402m) coordinating color

We used: Cascade Quatro (100% wool; 220 yards [201m] per 100g ball): #9435 (yarn A), 3 balls; Cascade 220 (100% wool; 220 yards [201m] per 100g ball): #8903 (yarn B), 2 balls

Needles: US size 13 (9mm) straight; US size 13 (9mm) double-pointed, set of 2

Notions: Tapestry needle; long sewing pins; 1½" (4cm) round button; craft knife; sewing needle and thread to match yarn

GAUGE

10 stitches and 14 rows = 4" (10cm) in stockinette stitch (before felting)

Notes
- Superwash wool and synthetics will not felt; do not use for felting projects.
- When changing colors, drop the old color and pick up the new color from under the old one, carrying the old color loosely upward along the side. This enables you to work the stripes without cutting the yarn.
- Use 2 strands of yarn held together as 1 throughout.

MAKE THE BAG

Holding 2 strands of yarn A together as 1 and using straight needles, loosely cast on 60 stitches.

Rows 1–5: Knit. At the end of row 5, drop yarn A (do not cut).

Row 6 (right side): Join yarn B (2 strands held together as 1), knit.

Row 7: Purl. Drop yarn B.

Row 8: Pick up yarn A, knit.

Row 9: Purl. Drop yarn A.

Rows 10–127: Repeat rows 6–9 until there are a total of 66 stripes, not counting the initial border (rows 1–5).

Rows 128 and 129: Repeat rows 6 and 7 for a 67th stripe.

Rows 130–134: Pick up yarn A and repeat rows 1–5.

Continuing with yarn A, loosely bind off 26 stitches, knit next 7 stitches (now there are 8 stitches total on the right needle, including the stitch remaining after bind-off), beginning with next 2 stitches bind off remaining 26 stitches to end of row.

MAKE THE BUTTON TAB

With wrong side facing, reattach yarn A (2 strands held together as 1) to edge of 8 stitches remaining on needle.

Row 1: Knit 1, purl 6, knit 1.

Row 2: Knit.

Rows 3–28: Repeat rows 1 and 2 thirteen times more.

Row 29: Repeat row 1.

Row 30: Knit.

Loosely bind off all stitches.

MAKE THE HANDLES (MAKE 2)

With 2 strands yarn A held together as 1 and using double-point needles, cast on 6 stitches leaving 8" (20.5cm) tail. Turn, and work in rows on 2 double-point needles as follows:

Rows 1–8: Knit.

Row 9: Knit 2 together, knit 2, knit 2 together. (4 stitches on needle)

Continue with 2 double-point needles and work 4-stitch I-cord for 25" (63.5cm).

Next row: Knit in front and back of first stitch, knit 2, knit in front and back of last stitch. Turn work. (6 stitches on needle)

Knit next 8 rows.

Loosely bind off all stitches, cut yarn leaving 8" (20.5cm) tail.

Repeat steps for second handle.

FINISHING

Fold body of bag in half with right sides together, bringing cast-on and bound-off edges together. Matching stripes, and using either yarn (2 strands held together) threaded on tapestry needle, whipstitch side seams together. Turn bag right side out. Pin each end of one handle to top edge of bag back, about 12 stitches in from each side seam. Pin each end of second handle to top edge of front of bag, about 12 stitches in from each side seam. Using the 8" (20.5cm) tail remaining from cast-on or bind-off threaded on tapestry needle, firmly whipstitch handles to bag body. Weave in all yarn ends to wrong side of work.

FELTING

Felt bag in washing machine (see Felting, page 34).

Add button

Once bag is dry, cut buttonhole in button tab using craft knife. Using sewing needle and thread, sew button to bag body beneath buttonhole.

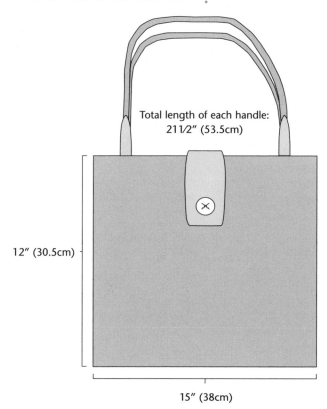

Total length of each handle:
21 1/2" (53.5cm)

12" (30.5cm)

15" (38cm)

Mittens and Headband

These mittens are cozy warm and easy to make. They are knit in the round, and the thumb is added at the end—almost an afterthought! Knit up a quick matching headband for a gift that will make anyone smile.

DESIGNER: LAURIE GONYEA

SIZE

Mittens
Hand length, from
  wrist to fingertips: 7" (18cm)
    Circumference: 7" (18cm)

Headband
    Circumference: 20" (51cm)
        Width: 3½" (9cm)

WHAT YOU'LL NEED

Yarn: Bulky weight wool yarn, about 109 yards [100m]; worsted weight curly mohair novelty yarn, about 75 yards [68.5m]

We used: Alafoss Lopi regular size (100% wool; 109 yards [100m] per 3½oz [100g] ball): #9738 Fire Red Tweed (yarn A), 1 ball; Kiperoo Farm Loop de Lou (100% mohair; about 75 yards [68.5m] per skein): multicolor (yarn B), 1 skein

Needles: US size 10½ (6.5mm) double-pointed, set of 5; US size 10½ (6.5mm) circular, 16" (40cm) long

Notions: Open-ring stitch markers; 24" (61cm) scrap smooth cotton yarn in contrasting color; tapestry needle

GAUGE
14 stitches and 20 rows = 4" (10cm)

MAKE THE MITTENS
Cuff
With double-point needles and 1 strand each yarn A and yarn B, cast on 24 stitches. Divide the stitches evenly between 4 needles (6 stitches on each needle). Join into a circle, taking care not to twist stitches. Place marker to denote beginning of round. Knit 5 rounds. Cut yarn B leaving 4" (10cm) tail. With yarn A,

knit 17 rounds (total of 22 rounds from cast-on edge).

Thumb marker round

Knit 1, drop yarn A; fold scrap cotton yarn in half and with both strands held together as 1, knit 4 stitches, drop scrap yarn; transfer the 4 scrap yarn stitches just knit back onto the left needle, pick up yarn A, reknit the 4 stitches, and complete the round. Knit 21 (total of 22 rounds from scrap yarn thumb stitches).

Shape mitten top

Round 1: (Knit 1, knit 2 together) to end of round. (16 stitches)

Rounds 2 and 3: Knit.

Round 4: (Knit 2 together) to end of round. (8 stitches)

Cut yarn leaving 8" (20.5cm) tail. Thread tail through tapestry needle and slip remaining stitches onto needle; pull tight and push needle to inside of mitten. Weave in tail to inside of work.

Thumb

With double-point needles pick up 9 stitches from below and above the scrap yarn thumb stitches as follows:

Needle #1: Pick up 1 stitch from the side and 2 of yarn A stitches from below the scrap yarn stitches.

Needle #2: Pick up next 2 yarn A stitches from below the scrap yarn and 1 stitch from the side.

Needle #3: Pick up 3 yarn A stitches from above the scrap yarn stitches.

Remove the scrap yarn. There should be 3 stitches on each of the 3 needles (9 stitches total).

Join yarn A, with needle #1 knit 1, make 1, knit remaining 2 stitches on needle; knit 2 stitches on needle #2, make 1, knit last stitch on needle; knit 3 stitches on needle #3 (11 stitches on 3 needles). Knit 11.

Shape thumb top

(Knit 2 together) 5 times, knit 1 (6 stitches remain). Cut yarn leaving 8" (20.5cm) tail. Thread tail through tapestry needle and slip remaining stitches onto needle; pull tight and push needle to inside of mitten. Weave in tail to inside of work. Close up any gaps on either side of thumb by weaving in ends from inside of mitten.

Repeat all steps for second mitten.

MAKE THE HEADBAND

With circular needle and yarn A, cast on 60 stitches. Place marker. Join the stitches into round, being careful not to twist them.

Round 1: Purl.

Rounds 2 and 3: Knit.

Join yarn B (do not drop yarn A) and knit 7 rounds with 2 yarns held together as 1. Cut yarn B, leaving tail to weave in later. Knit 2 rounds. Purl 1 round. Bind off all stitches. Weave in loose ends to wrong side of work.

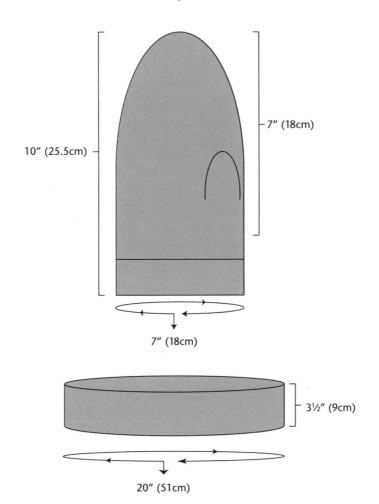

10" (25.5cm)

7" (18cm)

7" (18cm)

3½" (9cm)

20" (51cm)

Herringbone Belt

This stylish belt is simple to knit, with a combination of knits, purls, and slipped stitches that, combined with the suedelike yarn, creates an interesting texture. Close the belt by knotting the long fringes together around your waist.

DESIGNER: BETH WALKER-O'BRIEN

FINISHED SIZE

Width: 1.75" (4.4cm)

Length: 34" (86.5cm), not including fringe

WHAT YOU'LL NEED

Yarn: Worsted weight yarn, about 120 yards (110m)

We used: Berroco Suede Tri-Color (100% nylon; 120 yards [111m] per 50g ball): #3797 Django, 1 ball

Needles: US size 8 (5mm)

Notions: Size H/8 (5mm) crochet hook; tapestry needle

GAUGE

24 stitches and 55 rows = 4" (10cm) in pattern

Note: All stitches are slipped purlwise.

MAKE THE BELT

With crochet hook and tapestry needle, cast on 204 stitches using the crochet chain cast-on method.

Row 1 (right side): Slip 1 with yarn in front, with yarn in back knit 2, *slip 2 with yarn in front, with yarn in back knit 2; repeat from * until 1 stitch remains, knit 1.

Row 2: Slip 1 with yarn in front, purl 1, *slip 2 with yarn in back, with yarn in front purl 2; repeat from * until 2 stitches remain, purl 1, with yarn in back knit 1.

Row 3: Slip 3 with yarn in front, *with yarn in back knit 2, slip 2 with yarn in front; repeat from * until 1 stitch remains, with yarn in back knit 1.

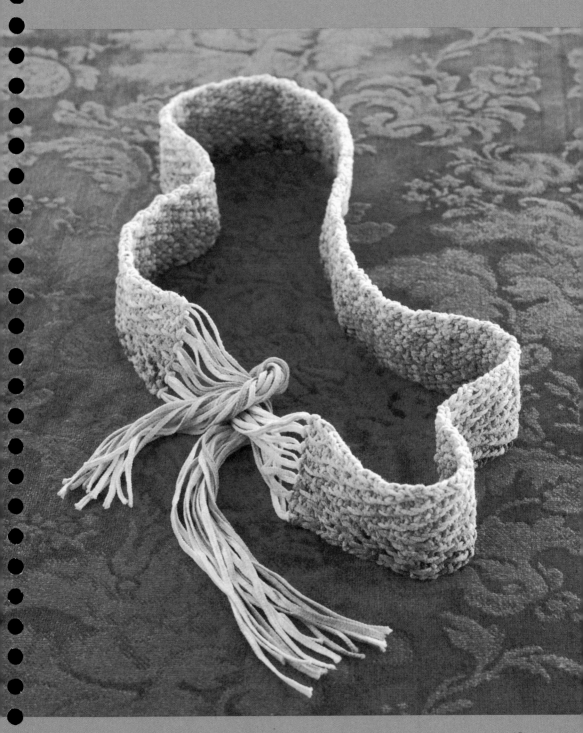

Row 4: Slip 1 with yarn in front, purl 3, *slip 2 with yarn in back, purl 2; repeat from * until 4 stitches remain, slip 2 with yarn in back, with yarn in front purl 1, knit 1.

Rows 5–12: Repeat rows 1–4 twice.

Row 13: Slip 3 with yarn in front, *with yarn in back knit 2, slip 2 with yarn in front; repeat from * until 1 stitch remains, with yarn in back knit 1.

Row 14: Slip 1 with yarn in front, purl 1, *slip 2 with yarn in back, with yarn in front purl 2; repeat from * until 2 stitches remain, purl 1, with yarn in back knit 1.

Row 15: Slip 1 with yarn in front, with yarn in back knit 2, *slip 2 with yarn in front, with yarn in back knit 2; repeat from * until 1 stitch remains, knit 1.

Row 16: Slip 1 with yarn in front, purl 3, *slip 2 with yarn in back, with yarn in front purl 2; repeat from * until 4 stitches remain, slip 2 with yarn in back, with yarn in front purl 1, with yarn in back knit 1.

Rows 17–20: Repeat rows 13–16.

Rows 21–23: Repeat rows 13–15.

Bind off while working row 16.

Weave in loose ends.

MAKE THE FRINGE

Make 14 fringes as follows: Cut fourteen 24" (61cm) strands of yarn. Place belt flat on table with right side facing. Beginning at one of the short edges, *insert crochet hook from back to front into the edge of the belt. Fold one strand in half and hold cut ends together to create a loop. Place loop on hook and pull it halfway through the knitted piece. With hook still in place, pull cut ends of fringe through the loop to make knot. Pull fringe ends to tighten. Repeat from * 6 more times, spacing fringe evenly along belt's edge. Repeat fringing at opposite end of belt. Trim all fringes to 11" (28cm) in length.

Curlicue Scarf

This fun and funky scarf is a blast to knit and so incredibly simple! The natural roll of stockinette stitch and a drastic increase in stitches causes the scarf to corkscrew around itself. It's cute as can be!

DESIGNER: BETH WALKER-O'BRIEN

Finished Size (After Blocking)
Width: 4" (10cm)

Length: 53" (134.5cm)

What You'll Need
Yarn: Bulky weight yarn, about 111 yards (101m) *each* in 2 colors; bulky weight waste yarn, about 5 yards (4.5m)

We used: Lion Brand Yarn Lion Suede Prints (100% polyester; 111 yards [101m] per 78g skein): #201 Canyon (color A), 1 skein; #202 Vineyard (color B), 1 skein

Needles: US size 9 (5.5mm) circular, 32" (81cm) long

Notions: Size I/9 (5.5mm) crochet hook; tapestry needle

Gauge
13 stitches and 22 rows = 4" (10cm) in stockinette stitch

Make the Scarf
With waste yarn, crochet hook, and circular needle, cast on 110 stitches using the crochet chain cast-on method.

Join color A:

Row 1 (right side): Knit.

Row 2: Purl.

Row 3: (Knit into front and back of stitch) until 1 stitch remains, knit 1. (219 stitches)

Row 4: Purl.

Row 5: (Knit into front and back of stitch) until 1 stitch remains, knit 1. (437 stitches)

Row 6: Purl.

Row 7: Knit.

Row 8: Purl.

Repeat rows 7 and 8 until piece measures 2" (5cm) from cast-on edge.

Bind off in pattern.

Remove waste yarn from crochet cast-on and place 110 stitches onto needle.

With purl side of color A facing, join color B and work rows 1–8.

Repeat rows 7 and 8 until piece measures 2" (5cm) from beginning of color B.

Bind off loosely. Weave in loose ends to wrong side of scarf.

FINISHING

Hand-wash in lukewarm water and mild soap, rinse, and press out excess water.

Shape to dry: Lay the scarf on a table. Starting at one of the short ends, twist the scarf clockwise so the 2 halves spiral around each other. While twisting the scarf, also roll the bound-off edges toward the knit side (they will naturally roll this way). Let dry.

Chevron Pillow

Fabulous colors, interesting texture, and a terrific pattern make this pillow a must-have accessory. Choose your own color palette and brighten up your home instantly. This quick-to-knit project makes a great gift.

DESIGNER: ANN BEREZ

FINISHED SIZE

15×15" (38×38cm)

WHAT YOU'LL NEED

Yarn: Bulky weight yarn in solid color (yarn A), about 100 yards (91.5m); bulky weight thick-and-thin yarn in multicolor (yarn B), about 300 yards (274m)

We used: Nashua Handknits Creative Focus Chunky (75% wool, 25% alpaca; 110 yards [100m] per 100g skein): #1450 blue pine (yarn A), 1 skein; Schaefer Yarns Elaine (100% merino wool; 300 yards [274m] per 8oz skein): Gertrude Ederle (yarn B), 1 skein

Needles: US size 10½ (6.5mm)

Notions: Stitch markers; long sewing pins; tapestry needle; 15" (38cm) square pillow form

GAUGE

14 stitches and 16 rows = 4" (10cm) in pattern

MAKE THE PILLOW

With yarn A, cast on 51 stitches.

Rows 1 and 2: Knit. Cut yarn leaving 4" (10cm) tail to weave in later.

Row 3 (right side): Join yarn B, knit 2, *knit into front and back of next stitch, knit 3, work slip slip knit decrease, knit 1, knit 2 together, knit 2, knit into front and back of next stitch**; repeat from * to ** 3 times more until 1 stitch remains, knit 1. Yarn B remains attached to work throughout project.

Row 4: With yarn B, knit 1, purl across row until 2 stitches remain, knit 2.

Rows 5, 7, and 9: Repeat row 3.
Rows 6, 8, and 10: Repeat row 4.

Repeat rows 1–10 eleven times more for a total of 120 rows, rejoining yarn A at the start of every row 1. Piece should measure about 30" (76cm).

Rejoin yarn A; knit 2 rows. Bind off with A. Cut yarns A and B leaving 4" (10cm) tails.

FINISHING

Weave in loose ends and block to size. Fold piece in half with wrong sides together and cast-on edge meeting bind-off edge. Pin in place, matching rows. With yarn A threaded on tapestry needle, sew sides together using mattress stitch. Insert pillow form; sew cast-on and bind-off edges together using mattress stitch.

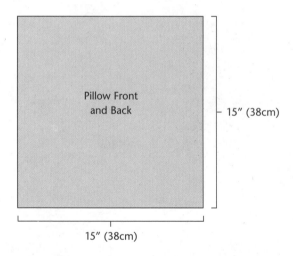

Pillow Front
and Back

15" (38cm)

15" (38cm)

Striped Wine Sack

A bottle of wine makes a nice gift, but presenting it in a one-of-a-kind hand-knit, felted wine sack makes a nice gift unforgettable.

DESIGNER: JUDITH HORWITZ

Size (after felting)

Length: Approximately 13½"
(34.5cm)

Circumference: Approximately 10"
(25.5cm)

Tie length: Approximately 50"
(127cm)

What You'll Need

Yarn: 100% wool worsted weight
yarn, about 175 yards
(160m)

We used: Noro Kureyon (100% wool;
109 yards per 50g ball):
color #154, 2 balls

Needles: US size 8 (5mm) double-
pointed, set of 4

Notions: Open-ring stitch marker;
tapestry needle; size I/9
(5mm) crochet hook

Gauge

15 stitches=4" (10cm) in circular
stockinette stitch (knit all rounds)

Note: Superwash wool and synthetics
will not felt; do not use for felting
projects.

Make the sack

Loosely cast 42 stitches onto one
double-point needle, then divide
stitches equally onto 3 needles
(14 stitches on each). Join into circle,
being careful not to twist stitches.
Place open-ring stitch marker in first
stitch to denote beginning of round,
and move marker upward every few
rounds.

Round 1 (wrong side): Knit.

Round 2 (right side): Purl.

Round 3: Knit.

Round 4: Purl.

Round 5: Knit.

Change to circular stockinette
stitch (knit all rounds) until piece
measures 17" (43cm).

Purl the next round (on right side of work).

Decrease rounds

Round 1: (Knit 5, knit 2 together) to end of round. (36 stitches)

Rounds 2, 4, 6, 8, and 10: Knit.

Round 3: (Knit 4, knit 2 together) to end of round. (30 stitches)

Round 5: (Knit 3, knit 2 together) to end of round. (24 stitches)

Round 7: (Knit 2, knit 2 together) to end of round. (18 stitches)

Round 9: (Knit 1, knit 2 together) to end of round. (12 stitches)

Round 11: (Knit 2 together) to end of round. (6 stitches)

Round 12: Knit. Remove marker.

Cut yarn leaving 6" (15cm) tail. Thread the tail onto a tapestry needle and pull through the remaining 6 stitches, pulling tightly to close. Weave in loose ends to wrong side of work.

MAKE THE TIE

With crochet hook and yarn, make a crochet chain about 56" (142cm) long. Beginning in second chain from hook work 1 single crochet in each chain to end of row. Fasten off.

FELTING

Felt wine sack and tie in washing machine (see Felting, page 34). The tie is finished felting when you can gently stretch it to about 50" (127cm). Let sack dry with wine bottle inside so it keeps its shape.

Tie overhand knot at both ends of strand, and tie around neck of wine bottle.

Ribby Socks

These funky socks feature a simple ribbing pattern that knits up quickly and shows off the beauty of handpainted yarn. A perfect first sock project!

DESIGNER: CHRISSY GARDINER

SIZE

Women's size medium

Instep circumference: 8" (20cm)

Cuff length: 6" (15cm)

Foot length: 9" (23cm)

WHAT YOU'LL NEED

Yarn: Worsted weight self-striping yarn, about 312 yards (285m)

We used: Artyarns Supermerino (100% superwash merino wool; 104 yards [95m] per 50g skein): #123, 3 skeins

Needles: US size 3 (3.25mm) double-pointed, set of 5

Notions: Open-ring stitch markers; tapestry needle

GAUGE

24 stitches and 32 rounds=4" (10cm) in circular stockinette stitch (knit every round)

MAKE THE SOCKS (MAKE 2)

Leg

Loosely cast on 50 stitches and divide onto 4 needles as follows: 12 stitches on needles #1 and #4 and 13 stitches on needles #2 and #3. Join stitches into a circle, being careful not to twist stitches. Place open-ring stitch marker in first stitch on needle #1 to denote beginning of rounds. Move marker upward every few rounds.

Note: Needles #1 and #4 will hold the heel stitches while needles #2 and #3 will hold the instep stitches.

Establish ribbing pattern as follows:

Round 1: Needle #1—purl 1, (knit 3, purl 2) two times, knit 1; needle #2—knit 2, (purl 2, knit 3) twice, purl 1; needle #3—purl 1, (knit 3, purl 2) twice, knit 2; needle #4—knit 1, (purl 2, knit 3) twice, purl 1.

Repeat round 1 until leg measures 6" (15cm).

Heel

Knit all stitches on needle #1. Turn work; purl all stitches on needles #1 and #4, working them all onto a single needle. These 24 stitches will form the heel flap.

Row 1 (right side): *Slip 1, knit 1; repeat from * 11 times more, turn.

Row 2: Slip 1, purl 23, turn work.

Repeat rows 1 and 2 fourteen times more (30 rows total).

Turn heel

Row 1: Knit 15, work slip slip knit decrease, turn work.

Row 2: Slip 1, purl 6, purl 2 together, turn work.

Row 3: Slip 1, knit 6, work slip slip knit decrease, turn work.

Row 4: Repeat row 2.

Repeat rows 3 and 4 until all heel stitches have been worked. There are now 8 heel stitches left.

Shape gusset

Turn work and knit the 8 heel stitches. With the same needle, pick up and knit 15 stitches along the right side edge of the heel flap. Work across stitches on needles #2 and #3 in ribbing pattern as established (26 instep stitches). With the empty needle, pick up and knit 15 stitches along the left side edge of the heel flap, then knit 4 stitches from needle #1. Place stitch marker in next stitch to denote beginning of rounds. The heel stitches should now be divided evenly on needles #1 and #4 (19 stitches on each), and 13 stitches remain on each of needles #2 and #3. (64 stitches total)

Round 1: Knit to last 3 stitches on needle #1, knit 2 together, knit 1. Work across needles #2 and #3 in ribbing pattern as established. At the beginning of needle #4, knit 1, work slip slip knit decrease, knit to end of needle.

Round 2: Knit all stitches on needle #1, work in established rib pattern on needles #2 and #3, knit all stitches on needle #4.

Repeat rounds 1 and 2 until there are 12 stitches on each of needles #1 and #4. There are now 50 stitches total.

Foot

Continue working the stitches on needles #2 and #3 in established rib pattern, and knit all stitches on needles #1 and #4 until the foot measures about 2" (5cm) shorter than desired finished length.

Shape toe using the star method as follows:

Round 1: *Knit to last 2 stitches on needle, knit 2 together; repeat from * across all needles.

Round 2: Knit all stitches.

Repeat rounds 1 and 2 until there are 2 stitches left on needles #1 and #4 and 3 stitches each on needles #2 and #3. (10 stitches total)

Next round: Needle #1—knit 2; needles #2 and #3—knit 1, knit 2 together; needle #4—knit 2. (8 stitches remain)

Remove marker. Break yarn and thread tail through remaining stitches. Pull tight to close toe. Weave in all yarn ends to wrong side of work.

Ripple Scarf

This gently waved scarf is worked vertically in Feather-and-Fan Stitch, the simplest knitted lace stitch. Made with a lusciously soft alpaca yarn, it's a treat for both the giver and receiver!

DESIGNER: BETH WALKER-O'BRIEN

FINISHED SIZE (AFTER BLOCKING)
Width: 4½" (11.5cm)
Length: 66" (167.5cm)

WHAT YOU'LL NEED
Yarn: Sport weight yarn, about 440 yards (402m)

We used: Blue Sky Alpacas Sport Weight (100% baby alpaca; 110 yards [100m] per 50g skein): #023 Red (color A), 1 skein; #211 Paprika (color B), 1 skein; #073 Tarnished Gold (color C), 1 skein; #046 Chartreuse (color D), 1 skein

Needles: US size 8 (5mm) circular, 32" (81cm) long

Notion: Tapestry needle

GAUGE (AFTER BLOCKING)
18 stitches and 26 rows = 4" (10cm) in pattern

MAKE THE SCARF
With color A, loosely cast on 308 stitches.

Row 1 (right side): Knit.

Row 2: Purl.

Row 3: Knit 1, *(knit 2 together) 3 times, (yarn over, knit 1) 6 times, (knit 2 together) 3 times; repeat from * to last stitch, knit 1.

Row 4: Knit.

Change to color B, repeat rows 1–4.
Change to color C, repeat rows 1–4.
Change to color D, repeat rows 1–4.
Change to color C, repeat rows 1–4.
Change to color B, repeat rows 1–4.
Change to color A, repeat rows 1–4.
Bind off loosely with color A.

Weave loose ends to wrong side of scarf, and block scarf to size.

Gull Stitch Toque

A toque is a close-fitting brimless hat that covers the ears.
Knitted toques are very much in style these days for both men
and women. At first glance this hat looks like it's knit in an
intricate cable pattern, but it is actually a simple slip-stitch
pattern—no cabling required!

DESIGNER: BETH WALKER-O'BRIEN

FINISHED SIZE

Circumference: 22" (56cm)
　　　　Height: 7" (18cm)

WHAT YOU'LL NEED

Yarn: Worsted weight yarn,
about 196 yards (180m);
smooth cotton waste yarn,
about 3 yards (2.75m)

We used: Karabella Yarns Aurora 8
(100% extrafine merino
wool; 98 yards [90m] per
50g ball): #4306, 2 balls

Needles: US size 8 (5mm) circular,
16" (40cm) long; US size
8 (5mm) double-pointed,
set of 5

Notions: US size H/8 (5mm) crochet
hook; open-ring stitch
markers; tapestry needle

GAUGE

23 stitches and 34 rows = 4" (10cm)
in Mock Gull Stitch pattern

Notes

- All stitches are slipped purlwise
with yarn in back.
- At the beginning of the hat, the
first set of the Mock Gull Stitch
pattern has been slightly modified
to prevent the cast-on edge from
scalloping.
- Once the decreases begin, change
to double-point needles when
necessary.

Make the hat

With waste yarn, crochet hook, and circular needle, cast on 128 stitches using crochet chain cast-on method.

Round 1: Join main yarn, *purl 2, knit 6; repeat from * to end of round. Join into circle being careful not to twist stitches. Place marker to denote beginning of round.

Round 2: (Slip 2, knit 2) to end of round.

Round 3: (Purl 2, knit 2, slip 2, knit 2) to end of round.

Round 4: (Slip 2, knit 2) to end of round.

Round 5: (Purl 2, knit 2, slip 2, knit 2) to end of round.

Round 6: *Purl 2, slip next 2 stitches to right needle, drop next stitch to front of work, slip the same 2 stitches back onto left needle, pick up dropped stitch, return it to left needle and knit it, knit 2, drop next stitch to front of work, knit 2, pick up dropped stitch, return it to left needle and knit it; repeat from * to end of round.

Round 7: (Purl 2, knit 6) to end of round.

Round 8: (Purl 2, knit 2, slip 2, knit 2) to end of round.

Rounds 9–11: Repeat round 8.

Round 12: Repeat round 6.

Rounds 13–42: Repeat rounds 7–12 five times more.

Round 43: (Purl 2, knit 6) to end of round.

Round 44 (decrease round): (Purl 2 together, knit 2, slip 2, knit 2) to end of round. (112 stitches on needle)

Round 45: (Purl 1, knit 2, slip 2, knit 2) to end of round.

Rounds 46 and 47: Repeat round 45.

Round 48 (decrease round): *Purl 1, slip next 2 stitches to right needle, drop next stitch to front of work, slip the same 2 stitches back onto left needle, pick up dropped stitch and return it to left needle and knit it; knit 2 together; drop next stitch to front of work, work slip slip knit decrease, pick up dropped stitch and return it to left needle and knit it; repeat from * to end of round. (80 stitches)

Round 49: (Purl 1, knit 4) to end of round.

Round 50: (Purl 1, knit 1, slip 2, knit 1) to end of round.

Rounds 51 and 52: Repeat round 50.

Round 53: *Purl 1, slip next stitch to right needle, drop next stitch to front of work, slip the same stitch back onto left needle, pick up dropped stitch and knit it, knit 1, drop next stitch to front of work, knit 1, pick up dropped stitch and knit it; repeat from * to end of round.

Round 54: (Purl 1, knit 4) to end of round.

Round 55 (decrease round): (Purl 1, work slip slip knit decrease, knit 2 together) to end of round.
(48 stitches)

Round 56: (Purl 1, knit 2) to end of round.

Round 57 (decrease round): (Purl 1, knit 2 together) to end of round.
(32 stitches)

Round 58: (Purl 1, knit 1) to end of round.

Round 59 (decrease round): (Knit 2 together) to end of round.
(16 stitches)

Round 60: Knit around.

Round 61 (decrease round): (Knit 2 together) to end of round.
(8 stitches)

Cut yarn and thread onto tapestry needle. Weave yarn tail through remaining 8 stitches on needle, gently pull to close top of hat.

Carefully remove waste yarn crochet cast-on, slipping 128 stitches onto circular needle. (Count stitches to be sure there are 128.)

Next round (right side): Join main yarn, (purl 2, purl 2 together) to end of round. (96 stitches)

Next round: Purl.

Bind off purlwise. Weave in loose yarn ends to wrong side of work.

Himalayan Silk Purse

This colorful purse is knit in three pieces and sewn together on the right side of the work to create a decorative ridged edge. The strap wraps along the edges and bottom, providing depth.

DESIGNER: BETH WALKER-O'BRIEN

FINISHED SIZE

Width: 6½" (16.5cm)

Height: 5½" (14cm) with flap closed, not including strap

WHAT YOU'LL NEED

Yarn: Heavy worsted weight yarn, about 80 yards (110m); worsted weight cotton waste yarn, about 1 yard (.9m)

We used: Himalaya Yarn Recycled Silk (100% silk; 80 yards [73m] per 100g skein): all assorted colors (no 2 hanks are exactly alike), 2 skeins

Needles: US size 7 (4.5mm)

Notions: Size G (4.25mm) crochet hook; 2 open-ring stitch markers; tapestry needle; stitch holder; long sewing pins; decorative button, approximately 1" (2.5cm) diameter

GAUGE

16 stitches and 38 rows = 4" (10cm) in Half Linen Stitch pattern

HALF LINEN STITCH

Note: All stitches are slipped purlwise. Slipping the first stitch in each row creates a chainlike selvage at each side of the work that will be used later when assembling the pieces.

Row 1 (wrong side): Slip 1 with yarn in front, *purl 1, slip 1 with yarn in back; repeat from * until 1 stitch remains, knit 1.

Row 2: Slip 1 with yarn in front, knit across.

Row 3: Slip 1 with yarn in front, *slip 1 with yarn in back, purl 1; repeat from * until 1 stitch remains, knit 1.

Row 4: Slip 1 with yarn in front, knit across.

MAKE THE FRONT

With crochet hook, needle, and main yarn, cast on 26 stitches using the crochet chain cast-on method. Work Half Linen Stitch pattern until piece measures 5½" (14cm) ending on wrong-side row.

Bind off all stitches loosely.

MAKE THE BACK

Work same as front until piece measures 5½" (14cm) ending on wrong-side row (do not bind off). Place an open-ring stitch marker at each side edge in this last row. Work next right-side row as follows: Slip 1 with yarn in front, slip slip knit decrease, work Half Linen Stitch pattern across row until last 3 stitches, knit 2 together, knit 1. (24 stitches remain)

Continue working in Half Linen Stitch pattern until piece measures 6.5" (16.5cm) from cast-on edge, ending with wrong-side row.

Begin decreases

Next right-side row: Slip 1 with yarn in front, slip slip knit decrease, knit across row until 3 stitches remain, knit 2 together, knit 1. (22 stitches)

Next wrong-side row: Continue in established Half Linen Stitch pattern.

Repeat the last 2 rows until 4 stitches remain.

Next right-side row: Knit 2 together, slip slip knit decrease, turn work. (2 stitches)

Next row (wrong side): Purl 2 together, cut yarn leaving at least a 12" (30.5cm) tail (tail will be used later to crochet-chain a loop to close around button), thread tail through remaining stitch and pull tail to tighten and secure stitch. Leave stitch markers in place until assembly is completed.

MAKE THE GUSSET (STRAP)

Note: The gusset is a knitted strip, 1" (2.5cm) wide, joined in a circle. It connects the front and back pieces of the purse and also serves as the purse strap.

With crochet hook, needle, and waste yarn, cast on 4 stitches using the crochet chain cast-on method.

With silk yarn and needle, work Half Linen Stitch pattern until piece measures 53½" (136cm) ending with wrong-side row. Cut yarn leaving 12" (30.5cm) tail and thread tail on tapestry needle. Seam gusset ends together as follows:

Remove waste yarn from cast-on edge and place the 4 stitches onto other needle. Holding the 2 needles parallel in your left hand, and with wrong sides of work held together, graft the stitches together using Kitchener stitch. You have now joined the gusset into a circle about 53½" (136cm) in circumference.

ASSEMBLE THE PURSE

Seam gusset to front piece as follows: With right sides facing, wrong side of purse front and one wrong side edge of gusset held together, pin gusset side edge along one 5½" (14cm) side edge of front, then along the 6½" (16.5cm) bottom edge, and then along the second 5½" (14cm) side edge of front, leaving the remaining 6½" (16.5cm) front top edge open. Thread tapestry needle with about a 20" (51cm) strand of main yarn. With right side of work facing and using backstitch, seam pieces together along the 3 pinned edges, joining one side edge of gusset to purse front. There should be about 36" (91.5 cm) of gusset

piece remaining free and unseamed (this will later serve as the shoulder strap). Rethread tapestry needle as necessary.

Cut yarn leaving 4" (10cm) tail, weave yarn tail through stitches on wrong side of gusset. Remove all pins.

Seam gusset to back as follows: With purse back and second side edge of gusset held together with wrong sides together, pin gusset to back, aligning back (beginning at one open-ring marker) along gusset edge to match the same length of gusset already seamed to purse front (see schematic on next page and assembled purse). Do not pin or sew the flap to gusset. Thread tapestry needle with about 20" (51cm) main yarn. Using backstitch, seam around 3 edges of back (ending at second open-ring marker). Cut yarn leaving 4" (10cm) tail, weave yarn tail through stitches on wrong side of gusset. Remove all pins and markers.

MAKE THE BUTTON LOOP

Using the 12" (30.5cm) tail at the top of triangular purse flap, crochet a chain long enough to fit around the button. Fasten the end of the chain to the first chain to form a loop. Fasten off yarn and using tapestry needle or crochet hook, weave loose end through several stitches on wrong side of purse flap. Sew button to front of purse, aligning with loop.

Weave in all loose ends.

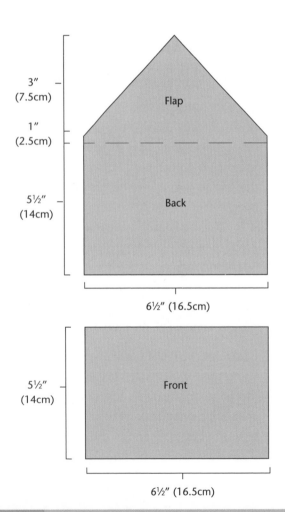

3" (7.5cm)

1" (2.5cm)

Flap

5½" (14cm)

Back

6½" (16.5cm)

5½" (14cm)

Front

6½" (16.5cm)

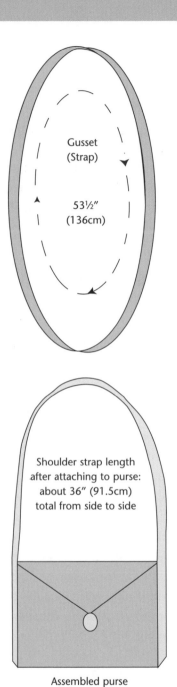

Gusset (Strap)

53½" (136cm)

Shoulder strap length after attaching to purse: about 36" (91.5cm) total from side to side

Assembled purse

Zigzag Throw

A handknit throw makes a cozy and thoughtful gift. The bulky chenille knits up quickly and comes in a dizzying array of colors: Just choose your favorites.

DESIGNER: BETH WALKER-O'BRIEN

FINISHED SIZE

Width: 37" (94cm)

Length: 43" (109cm)

WHAT YOU'LL NEED

Yarn: Bulky weight yarn, about 1,000 yards (914m)

We used: Lion Brand Yarns Chenille Thick & Quick (91% acrylic, 9% rayon; 100 yards [91.4m] per skein): #125 Chocolate (color A), 5 skeins; #108 Dusty Blue (color B), 5 skeins

Needles: US size 13 (9mm)

Notion: Tapestry needle

GAUGE

11 stitches and 16 rows = 4" (10cm) in Zigzag Stitch

ZIGZAG STITCH

Row 1 (right side): Slip 1 stitch purlwise with yarn in back, knit in front and back of next stitch, knit 4, slip slip knit decrease, knit 2 together, knit 4, *(knit in front and back of stitch) 2 times, knit 4, slip slip knit decrease, knit 2 together, knit 4; repeat from * until 2 stitches remain, knit in front and back of stitch, knit 1.

Row 2: Slip 1 purlwise with yarn in front, purl to end of row.

Row 3: Repeat row 1.

Row 4: Repeat row 2.

MAKE THE THROW

With color A, loosely cast on 100 stitches.

Begin with row 2 (wrong side) of pattern and work rows 2–4 of Zigzag Stitch pattern. After row 4 is finished, cut color A leaving 4" (10cm) tail to weave in later.

With color B, work rows 1–4 of Zigzag Stitch pattern. After row 4 is finished, cut color B leaving 4" (10cm) tail.

Continue working rows 1–4 of Zigzag Stitch alternating colors A and B until piece measures approximately 42" (104cm) from cast-on edge and last color worked is color B.

With color A, work rows 1–3 of Zigzag Stitch.

Bind off loosely purlwise.

MAKE THE TASSELS (MAKE 15)

For each tassel: Cut 6 strands of color A each 6" (15cm) long, cut 2 strands of color A each 9" (23cm) long, and cut 6 strands of color B each 6" (15cm) long. Holding all 12 of the 6" (15cm) strands together, tie them together at their midpoint with a 9" (23cm) strand of A. (Don't cut the ends of this strand; they will be used later to attach the tassels to the afghan points.) Fold the 12 strands in half at the tie and with remaining 9" (23cm) strand of A, tie them together approximately ½" (1cm) down from fold. Evenly trim strands at bottom of tassel.

Attach tassels to cast-on edge
Thread a tapestry needle with the remaining tails of a 9" (23cm) strand of color A and sew the tassel to one point along the cast-on edge of the throw. Repeat for each of the 6 remaining points.

Attach tassels to bind-off edge
Attach tassels same as for cast-on edge, attaching a tassel to each of the 6 points of the bound-off edge and at each of the 2 "half points" at the far right and far left side of the bound-off edge.

43" (109cm)

37" (94cm)

Checkered Pot Holders

The perfect gift for your favorite chef! These checkerboard pot holders are knitted using the intarsia technique and then felted in the washing machine to make them good and sturdy.

DESIGNER: CHRISSY GARDINER

SIZE

Before felting: about 11×13½" (28×34cm)

After felting: about 8×8½" (20×21.5cm)

WHAT YOU'LL NEED

Yarn: 100% wool worsted weight yarn, about 121 yards (111m) *each* in 2 colors (makes 2 pot holders)

We used: Knit Picks Wool of the Andes (100% wool; 110 yards [101m] per 50g skein): #23420 Coal (color A), 2 skeins; #23775 Fog (color B), 2 skeins

Needles: US size 8 (5mm) straight; US size 9 (5.5mm) double-pointed, set of 2

Notion: Tapestry needle

GAUGE

18 stitches and 24 rows=4" (10cm) in stockinette stitch before felting

Note: When changing colors, drop the old color and bring the new color up from under the old color, twisting them together to avoid gaps. For each section being worked, you will need 2 balls color A and 2 balls color B.

MAKE THE POT HOLDER

With color A and straight needles, loosely cast on 48 stitches.

Rows 1 and 2: Knit.

Row 3 (right side): With first ball of color A, knit 13, drop color A; attach first ball of color B, knit 11, drop color B; attach second ball of color A, knit 11, drop color A; attach second ball of color B, knit 11, drop color B; attach third ball of color A, knit 2, turn work.

Row 4: Still working with third ball of color A, knit 2, drop color A; pick up color B, purl 11, drop color B; pick up color A, purl 11, drop color A; pick up color B, purl 11, drop color B; pick up color A, purl 11, knit 2, turn work.

Rows 5–20: Repeat rows 3 and 4 eight times more.

Row 21: Repeat row 3 once more. Turn work. Cut all yarn except for the ball of color A that is at the working end of your needle.

Row 22 (wrong side): With attached ball of color A, knit 2, purl 11, drop color A; attach first ball of color B, purl 11, drop color B; attach second ball of color A, purl 11, drop color A; attach second ball of color B, purl 11, drop color B; attach third ball of color A, knit 2, turn work.

Row 23: Still working with third ball of color A, knit 2, drop color A; pick up color B, knit 11, drop color B; pick up color A, knit 11, drop color A; pick up color B, knit 11, drop color B; pick up color A, knit 13, turn work.

Rows 24–39: Repeat rows 22 and 23 eight times more.

Row 40: Repeat row 22 once more. Turn work. Cut all yarn except for the ball of color A that is at the working end of your needle.

Rows 41–78: Repeat rows 3–40 once more.

Rows 79 and 80: With attached ball of color A, knit all stitches.

Bind off all stitches very loosely. Weave in all yarn ends to wrong side of work.

MAKE THE HANGER

Using double-point needles and color A and leaving a 4" (10cm) tail at beginning, cast on 4 stitches. Work in I-cord for 6" (15cm); cut yarn leaving 4" (10cm) tail. With both yarn tails threaded on tapestry needle, stitch both ends of I-cord securely to upper left corner of pot holder to form a loop.

FELTING

Felt pot holders in washing machine (see Felting, page 34).

KEY

■ Color A: Knit on right side;
  purl on wrong side

▣ Color A: Knit on wrong side;
  purl on right side

☐ Color B

☐ Pattern repeat frame

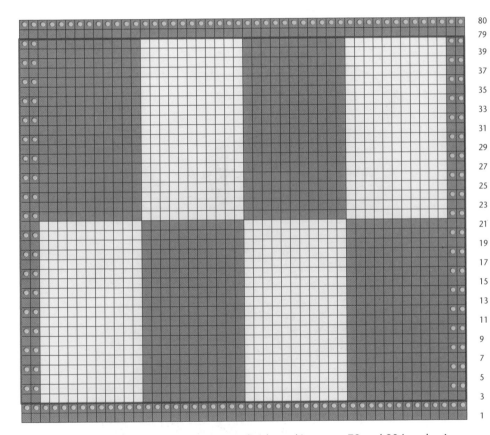

80
79
39
37
35
33
31
29
27
25
23
21
19
17
15
13
11
9
7
5
3
1

Work rows 1–40 once, 3–40 once more, finish working rows 79 and 80 in color A.

Mermaid Scarf

A quick and simple knit in a beautiful variegated silk-and-wool blend, this scarf features Mistake Rib Stitch, a pattern that looks great on both sides and doesn't curl. A strip of knitted fringe trim at the ends is fun and unusual.   DESIGNER: AMY POLCYN

Size

Approximately 5×60"
(12.5×152.5cm), including
knitted fringe

What You'll Need

Yarn: Worsted weight yarn,
about 327 yards (299m)

We used: South West Trading
Company Karaoke (50%
Soy Silk, 50% wool;
109 yards [100m] per 50g
ball): #278 Mermaid Mix,
3 balls

Needles: US size 7 (4.5mm)

Notion: Tapestry needle

Gauge

26 stitches and 30 rows=4" (10cm)
in pattern

Make the scarf

Loosely cast on 33 stitches.

Row 1: *Knit 2, purl 2; repeat from
* to last stitch, knit 1.

Row 2: *Purl 2, knit 2; repeat from
* to last stitch, purl 1.

Repeat rows 1 and 2 until scarf
measures 50" (127cm). Bind off
loosely in pattern.

Make the fringe (make 2)

Note: The fringe is worked from side
to side.

Loosely cast on 25 stitches.

Row 1: Knit.

Row 2: Knit.

Row 3: Loosely bind off 20 stitches
(1 stitch on right needle after bind-
off), knit 4. (5 stitches remain)

Row 4: Knit 5; using the backward
loop cast-on method, loosely cast on
20 stitches.

Row 5: Knit.

Row 6: Knit.

Row 7: Repeat row 3.

Repeat rows 4–7 seven times
more, then work rows 4–6 once
more. Bind off all 25 stitches loosely
(10 fringes).

With yarn threaded on tapestry
needle, whipstitch fringe to short end
of scarf.

Repeat fringe for other end of
scarf.

Weave in yarn ends to wrong side
of work. Lightly steam-block to
measurements.

Purl of Wisdom

When working in Mistake Rib
Stitch pattern, be sure to cast
on an odd number of stitches.

Mohair-look Hat

This quick and easy-to-knit luxurious hat fits most sizes. In just a couple of hours you will have a warm, soft-as-a-cloud headpiece you will treasure. The lower edge of the hat rolls up, adding a cute design element to a very simple piece. DESIGNER: SHIRLEY MACNULTY

SIZE

Diameter: approximately 18" (45.5cm) without stretching, 22" (56cm) with some stretching to fit head

Length (from top of crown to cast-on edge): about 9" (23cm)

WHAT YOU'LL NEED

Yarn: Worsted weight yarn, about 175 yards (160m)

We used: Mountain Colors Mohair (78% mohair,13% wool, 9% nylon; 225 yards [206m] per 3½oz [100g] skein): Ruby River (red hat), 1 skein; Coats & Clark Red Heart Symphony (100% acrylic; 310 yards [283m] per 3½oz [100g] ball): 4901 River Blue (blue hat), 1 ball

Needles: US size 9 (5.5mm) double-pointed, set of 4

Notions: Open-ring stitch marker; tapestry needle

GAUGE

14 stitches and 20 rows = 4" (10cm) in circular stockinette stitch

MAKE THE HAT

Cast on 60 stitches. Divide the stitches evenly among 3 needles (20 stitches on each needle). Join into a circle, being careful not to twist stitches. Place open-ring marker in first stitch to denote beginning of round, and move marker upward every few rounds. Work in circular stockinette stitch (knit every round) until hat measures 7½" (19cm) from cast-on edge.

Shape the crown

Round 1: (Knit 8, knit 2 together) to end of round. (54 stitches)

Round 2: (Knit 7, knit 2 together) to end of round. (48 stitches)

Round 3: (Knit 6, knit 2 together) to end of round. (42 stitches)

Round 4: (Knit 5, knit 2 together) to end of round. (36 stitches)

Round 5: (Knit 4, knit 2 together) to end of round. (30 stitches)

Round 6: (Knit 3, knit 2 together) to end of round. (24 stitches)

Round 7: (Knit 2, knit 2 together) to end of round. (18 stitches)

Round 8: (Knit 1, knit 2 together) to end of round. (12 stitches)

Round 9: (Knit 2 together) to end of round. (6 stitches)

Cut yarn leaving 12" (30.5cm) tail. Thread yarn tail onto tapestry needle and weave through 6 stitches of last round, pulling gently to close top. Cut yarn; weave in loose ends to wrong side of work.

Purl of Wisdom

Mohair yarn is ultra-soft, light, and airy. It is a joy to knit with. Because of its interesting texture, it's best to choose a simple pattern to show off the yarn to its best advantage.

Bulky Boot Socks

These socks are made for walking! This thick yarn knits up so quickly you'll have plenty of time to make extra pairs for everyone who falls in love with them.

DESIGNER: MEGAN LACEY

Size

Leg circumference: 9" (23cm)

Leg length (from cast-on to top of
heel flap): 9" (23cm)

Foot length (from heel to toe): 9"
(23cm)

What You'll Need

Yarn: Bulky weight wool yarn,
about 109 yards (100m)
color A; about 10 yards
(9m) color B; about
35 yards (32m) color C

We used: Alafoss Lopi regular size
(100% wool; 109 yards
[100m] per 3½oz ball):
#0005 Charcoal (color A),
1 ball; #0057 Gray (color
B), 1 ball; #0051 Cream
(color C), 1 ball

Needles: US size 7 (4.5mm) double-
pointed, set of 4

Notions: Open-ring stitch markers;
stitch holder; tapestry
needle

Gauge

17 stitches and 20 rounds = 4" (10cm)
in stockinette stitch

Make the sock (make 2)

With color C (cream) cast on
40 stitches. Divide stitches as follows:
14 stitches on first needle, 12 on
second, and 14 on third. Join stitches
into a circle, being careful not to
twist stitches, and place marker in
first stitch to denote beginning of
round. Work in knit 1, purl 1 ribbing
for 10 rounds. Change to circular
stockinette stitch (knit all rounds) for
10 rounds. Begin chart A.

Note: When knitting from charts,
always read rounds right to left and
carry yarn not in use loosely behind
work.

Work 4 rounds following chart A,
changing colors as shown on chart.
When chart A is completed, cut
colors B (gray) and C (cream) leaving
4" (10cm) tails to weave in later.
Continue to knit all rounds with color
A (charcoal) until sock measures 8"
(20.5cm) from cast-on edge.

Make heel

Slip last 12 stitches of last round and knit first 10 stitches of next round onto 1 needle (22 heel flap stitches), leaving 18 stitches on 2 needles for instep stitches. Slip these 18 stitches onto stitch holder.

Row 1: Working with the 22 heel flap stitches, (purl 2 together, purl 2) 5 times, purl 2. (17 stitches)

Row 2: (Knit 1, slip 1) to last stitch, knit 1.

Row 3: Knit 1, purl to last stitch, knit 1.

Repeat rows 2 and 3 until heel measures 2" (5cm), ending with a wrong-side row.

Next row (right side): Knit 7, knit 2 together, knit 8. (16 stitches)

Begin short rows for heel shaping

Row 1: Purl 8, purl 2 together, purl 1, leave remaining 5 stitches unworked on left needle, turn work.

Row 2: Knit 3, work slip slip knit decrease, knit 1, leave remaining 4 stitches unworked on left needle, turn work.

Row 3: Purl 4, purl 2 together, purl 1, leave remaining 3 stitches on left needle, turn work.

Row 4: Knit 5, work slip slip knit decrease, knit 1, leave remaining 2 stitches on left needle, turn work.

Row 5: Purl 6, purl 2 together, purl 1, leave remaining stitch on left needle, turn work.

Row 6: Knit 7, work slip slip knit decrease, knit 1, turn work.

Row 7: Purl 10.

Row 8: Knit 10.

With right side facing and using spare needle, pick up 11 stitches along side of heel flap. Slip 18 instep stitches from stitch holder onto an empty needle, with second needle knit across the 18 instep stitches, keeping them on 1 needle.

With third needle pick up 11 stitches along other side of heel flap and then knit 5 stitches from needle holding the heel stitches. Place marker after these 5 stitches and before the next 5 stitches to denote beginning of round. Transfer the remaining 5 heel stitches (those in front of the stitch marker) onto first needle. (There are now 16 stitches on first needle, 18 on second needle, and 16 on third needle for a total of 50 stitches.)

Round 1: First needle—knit to last 3 stitches, knit 2 together, knit 1; second needle—knit; third needle—knit 1, work slip slip knit decrease, knit to end of round. (48 stitches)
Round 2: Knit.

Repeat these 2 rounds 4 times more. (40 stitches remain)

Continue to knit in rounds until foot measures about 5½" (11.5cm) from heel. (To alter size, knit in rounds until sock foot measures 3½" [9cm] short of desired length.) Work chart B, changing colors as shown on the chart. When chart B is completed, cut colors A (charcoal) and B (gray) leaving 4" (10cm) tails to weave in later. With color C (cream) knit 1 round.

Shape toe

Continuing with color C, divide the 40 foot stitches as follows: 10 stitches on first needle, 20 on second, and 10 on third.

Round 1: First needle—knit to last 3 stitches, knit 2 together, knit 1; second needle—knit 1, work slip slip knit decrease, knit to last 3 stitches, knit 2 together, knit 1; third needle—knit 1, work slip slip knit decrease, knit to end.
Round 2: Knit.

Repeat these 2 rounds 6 times more for a total of 14 rounds. (12 stitches remain)

Knit stitches from first needle onto third needle so there are 6 stitches on each of 2 needles. Cut yarn C leaving 20" (51cm) tail, thread tail on tapestry needle and graft toe stitches together with Kitchener stitch.

FINISHING

Weave in loose ends to wrong side of work. Lay flat and block with damp cloth.

Purl of Wisdom
Leg- and foot-lengths are adjustable without changing stitch count. Simply add more rows where needed.

KEY

Knit all stitches every round in colors as shown.

■ Charcoal, color A

▨ Gray, color B

□ Cream, color C

□ Pattern repeat frame

Chart A

begin round

Chart B

begin round

Bias Bag

This is the bag you've been dreaming of! Two sumptuous yarns knit on the bias combine to make this classic design unforgettable.

DESIGNER: LUCIE SINKLER

SIZE

Bag: 10×10" (25.5×25.5cm)

Strap: 28" (71cm) long

WHAT YOU'LL NEED

Yarn: Silk/rayon blend yarn, worsted weight, about 300 yards (274m); 100% cotton sport weight yarn (use doubled), about 230 yards (210m)

We used: Indra silk (70% silk, 30% viscos; about 300 yards [274m] per 7½oz juggle ball): all assorted colors—no 2 balls are exactly alike (yarn A), 1 skein; Zitron Samoa (100% cotton; 115 yards [105m] per 50g skein): #38 (yarn B), 2 skeins

Needles: US size 8 (5mm)

Notions: Long sewing pins; tapestry needle

GAUGE

16 stitches and 32 rows = 4" (10cm)

Notes

- This purse is knitted in garter stitch (knit every row) placed on the bias. We used 2 yarns and alternated them every 2 rows. You will start knitting in 1 corner of the body, first creating a triangle, then knit on an angle to complete a rectangle knitted on the bias.
- When working with yarn B, use 2 strands held together as 1.
- The strap is knitted separately and stitched in place.

MAKE THE BAG

Section 1

With yarn A, cast on 3 stitches.

Row 1: Knit.

Row 2: Knit into front and back of next 2 stitches, knit 1. (5 stitches)

Row 3: Knit.

Row 4 (right side): With 2 strands held together as 1, join yarn B (do not cut yarn A). With yarn B, knit into front and back of first stitch, knit 2, knit into front and back of next stitch, knit 1. (7 stitches)

Row 5: Knit.

Row 6: With yarn A, knit into front and back of first stitch, knit 4, knit into front and back of next stitch, knit 1. (9 stitches)

Row 7: Knit.

Row 8: With yarn B, knit into front and back of first stitch, knit 6, knit into front and back of next stitch, knit 1. (11 stitches)

Row 9: Knit.

Continue in striped pattern, increasing on first and second-to-last stitches until there are 51 stitches on needle. End with wrong-side row (all knit, no increases).

Section 2

Maintaining established striped pattern, continue as follows:

Row 1 (right side): Knit into front and back of first stitch, knit 48, knit 2 together.

Row 2: Knit.

Repeat these 2 rows, changing colors every 2 rows until piece measures 21" (53.5cm) from cast-on corner. End with row 2.

Section 3

Maintaining established striped pattern, continue as follows:

Next row: Work slip slip knit decrease, knit across row until 2 stitches remain, knit 2 together.

Row 2: Knit.

Repeat these 2 rows until 3 stitches remain. Bind off loosely.

MAKE THE STRAP

With 2 strands of yarn B held together as 1, cast on 8 stitches. Work in garter stitch (knit every row) until strap measures 48" (122cm). Bind off loosely.

FINISHING

Fold body of purse in half with right sides together. The straight edge with 3 bind-off stitches and the straight edge with 3 cast-on stitches are together at the opposite end from the folded edge, forming the bag opening. Mark across fold line with pins. Unfold bag. Match center of strap cast-off edge to marked fold line on bag. Pin in place. With 1 strand of yarn B threaded on tapestry needle, sew together using backstitch. Pin strap to matching edges and sew in place. Repeat for cast-on edge of strap on other side of purse. Weave in loose ends to wrong side of purse. Turn purse to right side. Remove all pins.

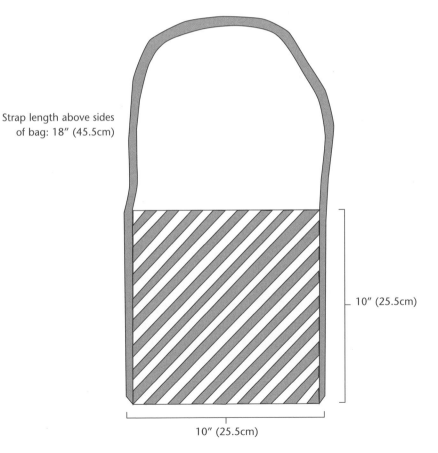

Strap length above sides of bag: 18" (45.5cm)

10" (25.5cm)

10" (25.5cm)

Fluffy Fun Pillows

Relax, and let the yarn do all the work on these fast and fun-to-knit pillows. With these terrific yarns you'll find a combo to match any color scheme. Knitting the round pillow is a perfect way to become comfortable with double-point needles.

DESIGNER: VANESSA MONTILEONE

SIZE

Round pillow: 12" (30.5cm) diameter
Square pillow: 11½×11½"
    (29×29cm)
Note: Knitted pieces will stretch to fit standard-size pillow forms.

WHAT YOU'LL NEED

Yarn: *For each pillow:* Machine-washable light worsted weight or DK weight microfiber yarn, 150 yards (137m); 3-color self-stripping novelty yarn, 57 yards (52m) in colors to coordinate with microfiber yarn; *for round pillow (side 2 only):* solid-color novelty yarn in color to coordinate with other yarns, 64 yards (58m)

We used: For each pillow: Lion Brand Yarn Micro Spun (100% microfiber acrylic; 168 yards [154m] per 70g skein): #147 purple (yarn A), 1 skein; Lion Brand Yarn Fun Fur Stripes (100% polyester; 57 yards [52m] per 40g ball): #300 Cotton Candy (yarn B), 1 ball. *For round pillow side 2:* Lion Brand Yarn Fun Fur (100% polyester; 64 yards [58m] per 50g ball): #191 violet (yarn C), 1 ball

Needles: *Square pillow*—US size 9 (5.5mm)
Round pillow—US size 9 (5.5mm) double-pointed, set of 5; US size 9 (5.5mm) circular, 24" (61cm) long

Notions: Tapestry needle; open-ring stitch marker; 12×12" (30.5×30.5cm) square pillow form *or* polyester fiberfill stuffing; round pillow form about 12" (30.5cm) diameter

GAUGE

14 stitches and 20 rows = 4" (10cm) in stockinette stitch with 2 yarns held together as 1. *Note:* Exact gauge is not needed for these pillows.

MAKE THE SQUARE PILLOW

Note: To allow for easier seaming, all edge stitches of the square pillow are knit with yarn A only.

Cast on 40 stitches with yarn A.

Row 1: Knit.

Row 2: Purl.

Row 3 (right side): Knit 2, join yarn B and with 2 yarns held together as 1 knit 36, drop yarn B (do not cut), knit 2.

Row 4 (wrong side): With yarn A only, knit 2, pick up yarn B and with 2 yarns held together as 1 purl 36, drop yarn B (do not cut), purl 2.

Repeat rows 3 and 4 until piece measures 11" (29cm) or to end of yarn B, ending with wrong-side row.

Drop yarn B and with yarn A only, knit 1 row. Purl the next row. Bind off loosely.

Repeat all steps for back of pillow.

FINISHING

Weave in loose ends to wrong side of work. With yarn A threaded on tapestry needle, and right sides together, whipstitch the pieces together on 3 sides, being sure to align the stripes. Insert pillow form or stuff with fiberfill. To close top seam, whipstitch across the yarn A edge stitches, pushing them to wrong side of work as you sew.

MAKE THE ROUND PILLOW

Note: Both pieces of the round pillow are worked in circular stockinette stitch (knit all rounds). Increases are made by knitting into the front and back of the stitch.

Side 1

With yarn A and yarn B held together as 1 and using double-point needles, cast on 8 stitches. Divide stitches evenly onto 4 needles, and join into a circle, being careful not to twist stitches. Place marker to note beginning of round. Change to circular needles when increased stitch numbers no longer fit comfortably on double-point needles.

Round 1: Knit.

Round 2: (Knit into front and back of stitch) 8 times. (16 stitches)

Rounds 3 and 4: Knit.

Round 5: *Knit 1, knit into front and back of next stitch; repeat from * to end of round. (24 stitches)

Rounds 6 and 7: Knit.

Round 8: Repeat round 5. (36 stitches)

Rounds 9–11: Knit.

Round 12: Repeat round 5. (54 stitches)

Rounds 13–15: Knit.

Round 16: *Knit 2, knit into front and back of next stitch; repeat from * to end of round. (72 stitches)

Rounds 17–19: Knit.

Round 20: Repeat round 16. (96 stitches)

Rounds 21–24: Knit.

Round 25: *Knit 3, knit into front and back of next stitch; repeat from * to end of round. (120 stitches)

Rounds 26–29: Knit.

Rounds 30–31: Drop yarn B; knit rounds using yarn A only.

   Bind off loosely.

Side 2

Repeat all steps to make back of pillow, using yarns A and C only.

FINISHING

Weave in loose ends to wrong side of work. With right sides together, seam the pieces together around the outer edges using backstitch, leaving the top one-third open. Turn pillow right side out, insert pillow form or stuff with fiberfill and close remaining one-third with whipstitch.

Designer Directory

Ann Berez
CloseKnit, Inc.
622 Grove St.
Evanston, IL 60201
Phone: (847) 328-6760

Chrissy Gardiner
Gardiner Yarn Works
Portland, OR
Phone: (503) 922-0168
www.gardineryarnworks.com
e-mail:
cgardiner@gardineryarnworks.com

Laurie Gonyea
Destination Knits
3419 Morrison St. NW
Washington, D.C. 20015
www.destinationknits.com
e-mail: destinationknits@yahoo.com

Judith Horwitz
CloseKnit, Inc.
622 Grove St.
Evanston, IL 60201
Phone: (847) 328-6760

Megan Lacey
Lacey's Wool Gathering
391 Carnegie Beach Rd.
Scugog Island, ON L9L 1B6
Canada
www.laceyswoolgathering.com
e-mail: laceyswoolgathering@sympatico.ca

Shirley MacNulty
Wilmington and Sugar Mountain, NC
Phone: (828) 260-1859
e-mail: baycountry@bellsouth.net

Vanessa Montileone
Yarning to Knit
Phone: (417) 886-8018
Fax: (417) 886-8709
e-mail: knitfast1@aol.com

Amy Polcyn
Phone: (734) 266-1566
http://frottez.blogspot.com
e-mail: apolcyn@att.net

Lucie Sinkler
CloseKnit, Inc.
622 Grove St.
Evanston, IL 60201
Phone: (847) 328-6760
Fax: (847) 328-0618
e-mail: closeknit@sbcglobal.net

Beth Walker-O'Brien
Knits Illustrated
Phone: (630) 841-3360
www.knitsillustrated.com
e-mail: beth@knitsillustrated.com